HOW TO SUF

In this Series

Other titles in preparation

How To...

SURVIVE DIVORCE

A handbook of guidance and practical advice

Roy van den Brink-Budgen

Second edition

How To Books

British Library Cataloguing-in-Publication data
A catalogue record for this book is available from the British Library.

© Copyright 1990 and 1995 by Roy van den Brink-Budgen

Published by How To Books Ltd, Plymbridge House, Estover Road,
Plymouth PL6 7PZ, United Kingdom.
Tel: Plymouth (01752) 735251/695745. Fax: (01752) 695699. Telex: 45635.

First published 1990
Second edition (revised and updated) 1995

Note: The material contained in this book is set out in good faith for general
guidance and no liability can be accepted for loss or expense incurred as a
result of relying in particular circumstances on statements made in the book.
The laws and regulations are complex and liable to change, and readers
should check the current position with the relevant authorities before making
personal arrangements.

Typeset by Kestrel Data, Exeter
Printed and bound in Great Britain by
The Cromwell Press, Broughton Gifford, Melksham, Wiltshire.

Contents

LIST OF ILLUSTRATIONS

Preface

to the Second Edition

If present trends continue, about one third of all marriages will end in divorce; that adds up to a lot of husbands, wives, and children. It also adds up to a lot of anger, confusion, and stress—and, of course, to a lot of money spent on lawyers to take apart what clergy and registrars have put together.

Most people find themselves unprepared for what is involved. They do not anticipate what the breakdown of their marriage can mean. The effects are experienced in varying degrees by everyone involved, as the shock waves engulf children, relatives, and friends.

Solicitors can help take you through all the legal stages of this process, but most people need much more than just legal guidance. They also need help in sorting out the emotional upheaval which accompanies separation. They may need help in deciding what to do with the children. They may need help in working out what choices they can make and how to make them. Above all, they need to be able to consider the long-term as well as the immediate implications of their actions.

This book is intended to meet those needs. Fully revised and updated to take account of the Child Support Agency and other legal changes, it offers practical advice on the sort of problems and experiences associated with divorce. It stresses the importance of analysing your own problems and, through this analysis, discovering how to overcome them.

It also aims to ask and answer questions on many of the legal aspects of divorce, including residence, contact, and maintenance. It provides details of other sources of help: counselling and conciliation services, agencies dealing with debt and housing problems, and organisations which seek to provide an opportunity for you to meet people in a similar situation to your own. The aim of this book, then, is to help you survive your divorce. It cannot make divorce painless but hopefully it will contribute to reducing the level of pain and confusion.

A number of case studies have been used to illustrate the book.

Although the experiences shown are based on true life, all the characters are entirely fictional and the creation of the author. For me, the pain and confusion have been greatly reduced by my family. They have turned darkness into light, confusion into certainty. For every reason I must thank my wife, Annie. Without her support, understanding, kindness, and love, I could not begin to put pen to paper. My children, Simon, Petra, Ruth, Adam, and Roy are to be thanked both together and separately for turning me into a happy man.

Roy van den Brink-Budgen

1
Surviving Apart

THINKING ABOUT DIVORCE

No one should think of setting off across the Atlantic on a single-handed yacht race without very careful preparation. This advice is obvious because no one would embark on such a trip without a thorough understanding of navigation and the techniques of sailing. So why do so many people set out on the road to divorce without similar thorough preparation? No one should underestimate what is involved.

● There are higher rates of both physical and mental illness during and following separation and divorce.
● There can be problems of accommodation.
● There can be problems of debt.
● Job performance may be affected.
● Alcohol consumption tends to increase.

Separation and divorce, then, can be responsible for many problems—but remember, you are not the only one experiencing such problems.

The statistics

● Britain has the second highest divorce rate of all the countries in the European Union; only Denmark is higher.
● Nearly 200,000 couples in Britain will divorce this year.
● About one third of all current marriages, on present trends, will end in divorce.
● 40 per cent of first marriages are likely to end in divorce.
● The average length of a marriage which ends in divorce is ten years but one third of all divorces take place within the first five years.
● About 2,000,000 children under 16 are affected and each year another 160,000 are involved.
● One child in five will see his or her parents divorce.

- 32 per cent of children of divorcing couples are under 5, a proportion which is steadily growing.
- Three quarters of those who divorce remarry (although there is an increasing proportion who do not).
- Second marriages seem twice as likely to end in divorce as first marriages.
- It is estimated that divorce costs this country at least £2,000 million each year in legal bills, social security benefits, health care and so on.

Divorce, then, is not just a problem for you as an individual; it is a major social problem. As well as affecting the couple involved and their children, it can also affect the parents of the couple (both as parents and as grandparents), other relatives, friends of the couple and of the children, and colleagues at work.

UNDERSTANDING WHY MARRIAGES BREAK UP

There is no single recipe for success in marriage. Marriages are made and broken for many reasons and, though we cannot be sure which marriage will last and which will not, we know that there are some things which make a marriage more vulnerable. A higher risk of divorce is associated with all of the following:

- marrying young
- the woman being pregnant before marriage
- unemployment—this doubles the risk
- parental opposition to the marriage
- lack of contact with one or both sets of parents
- problems with accommodation
- very short courtship
- redundancy and early retirement
- a history of truancy

Of course, it would be wrong to suggest that if one or more of the above are present in a marriage divorce will be inevitable; but it *is* true that any of the above factors makes a marriage a little more vulnerable to breaking down. Marrying young, for example, increases the risk of divorce—partly because people change as they grow older. Someone at 18 is likely to be a different person when they're 25. So if you marry at 18, both you and your partner are going to be married to different people, so to speak, by the time you are 25.

Having disappointed expectations

When people get married, they have expectations of what life with their partner is going to be like. When people get divorced, at least one of the partners must have been disappointed; the marriage did not fulfil their expectations. So, the greater the expectations, the higher the risk of being disappointed.

People probably have greater expectations of marriage than they did, say, 50 years ago. Married couples expect to be, and remain good friends, they probably expect a good standard of living, and they expect that having children will be a fulfilling and rewarding experience.

On their wedding day, the couple are good friends, probably surrounded by people who, by their gifts and good wishes, reinforce the feeling that all will be well. A year later, they may not be such good friends. Perhaps they lack companionship, or are bored, and they may be wondering what went wrong. The expectations were not fulfilled. Married life has become a series of sometimes small, sometimes large irritations. The couple have grown apart.

Case study: Di and Nick

Di and Nick have been married for just over a year. 'It was a huge wedding,' explains Di. 'My mother wanted me to have a fairy tale wedding. ''Just like a princess'', she said. The trouble is that that makes it much more difficult to admit that Nick and I should never have got married in the first place. My parents spent thousands on the wedding, and for what? For Nick and I to get divorced?

'I suppose it *was* a bit like a fairy tale. We'd been going out with each other since we were at school. Since we were 14, actually. It's awful, isn't it? For eight years, we've been Di and Nick, always together. And that was the problem, if you like. By the time we got married, it was as if I'd been married to him for years. I wasn't the little girl that my father thought he was walking down the aisle. I wasn't the princess my mother could see. I was a bored married woman, tired of being Di and Nick. I wanted to be somebody else.

'And that's been the problem all along. I should never have married Nick. But trying to work out why I should upset everybody by leaving him, that's the thing that's difficult. I can just imagine what my mother would say. ''The trouble with you, Diane, is that you expect too much. It's not as if he knocks you about or anything.''

'I don't think I do expect too much. I just want my husband to be my best friend, somebody who'll make me feel really good. I mean, really good. And I want him to feel really good when he's with me. That's what you should feel when you're married, isn't it?'

Growing apart

Growing apart is not, of course, inevitable. People can change in a marriage and, in doing so, grow together. People can mature and develop along the same lines. But, if you are considering separation and divorce, presumably you have already grown apart. How this has happened and the extent of your differences will inevitably depend on your particular case—but if at all possible, you should at least try to *analyse* what has gone wrong before you consider separation.

DECIDING TO SEPARATE

The decision to separate is one of the most important decisions that you will ever take in your life. So, the first rule for survival is:

- *Do not underestimate the seriousness of separation.*

Remember—it is much easier to get married than to go through the process of separation and divorce. It is more than just a change of address or even a change of partner—it is a change in the whole direction of your life. Ask yourself: Who will you become afterwards? Who will your children become?

Very often, when two people are separating, they reach a point when neither knows what he or she wants to do. This applies especially to the person who is leaving. Doubts and uncertainties begin to cloud your judgement. When this happens, you can make mistakes that you are likely to regret for a long time. Only when you are *clear* about your own feelings can you fully benefit from the advice in this book on such matters as children, property, debts and so on.

So, every time you falter or are troubled, ask yourself the questions below, answer them, and look at what your answers are telling you. Do you go back? Do you stay separated? Do you go for a divorce? These questions are probably too large for you to answer immediately. Try beginning with some smaller scale questions; answer these first and you'll find it easier to answer the big ones later. There are no right or wrong answers, just answers that are appropriate to you. It is up to you then to interpret your answers—to work out what they are telling you.

Your spouse's good points
Does your spouse:

- excite you?
- make you laugh?
- act as a good friend to you?
- behave generously?
- show you tenderness?
- make you feel proud when you are out together?

Your spouse's bad points
Does your spouse:

- bore you?
- behave inconsiderately?
- belittle you?
- show little interest in you?
- act irresponsibly or extravagantly?
- behave in a mean way?

General questions about your spouse

- Do the good points outweigh the bad?
- Would you like to spend the day alone with your spouse?
- Would you like to spend a weekend away together? Would you find it wonderful/very good/good/OK/not unpleasant/boring/too long/unthinkable?
- How long ago was it that you really missed him/her?
- If you couldn't see them for six months, would you miss him/her?
- What would be the bad points about not seeing him/her?
- What would be the good points?
- If s/he was not your spouse, would you want him/her to be?
- Do you like your spouse?
- Would you sacrifice yourself for him/her?
- Do you want him/her to remain an important part of your life?

Some of these questions may seem pretty obvious, but it is surprising how many people go into a separation or divorce before they have asked themselves the most obvious questions. Sit down, and try to think rationally about your situation.

Your new partner
If you have a new partner, ask the same questions about him or her.

What do the answers tell you about your relationship with your new partner? Contrast your answers for your spouse and for your new partner. What does the contrast tell you?

If your spouse is leaving

● Does your spouse have good reasons for going?
● If so, what are they?
● If not, why is your spouse leaving?
● Have you got good reasons for wanting him/her to stay?
● What are they?
● If things have gone wrong, why should they get better?
● Are there any positive aspects to the fact that your spouse is leaving?
● What are they?

Ultimately the question is not 'Why should we split up?' but rather 'Why should we stay together?' The aim of these questions is to get you to clarify your own feelings and your own position. Once you are clear about your position, then you can usefully tackle the 'nitty gritty' of property, money, the arrangements for the children, and so on. The questions should help you to distinguish your feelings about your spouse from those about your children, your home, your bank balance or whatever. *It is your relationship with your spouse that you need to be clear about first of all*; children grow up and leave, bank balances can heal, another home can be established.

Thinking about the children

The problem of any children involved has been deliberately omitted at this stage. You are not married to them and your feelings about them need to be kept distinct from your feelings about your spouse. If you decide to get back together for the sake of the children (and only for this reason), then you may be merely postponing separation and divorce. The tensions, dissatisfactions, irritations, anger, disappointments, and resentments are all still there. The children cannot be expected to make them go away. It's not their job and it's unfair to put the burden of creating happiness on to them. Children are likely to be happier in a 'clean' divorce than in a family which stays together unhappily. So although you should not underestimate the impact of separation and divorce, it is equally important not to underestimate the impact of an unhappy marriage. Children will be dealt with in more detail in Chapter 5.

If you have been growing apart in your marriage, it may be best to approach divorce as the method by which growing apart is completed. The rest of this book will help you to do this. To survive divorce, you must be realistic about both **what you are giving up** and **what you are going to do next.**

What are you giving up?

Whether you are the leaver or the one who has been left, make a list of all the things you will have to do without. It should include the following (which are not given in any order of importance: this will depend upon you):

● house
● income
● possessions (furniture, car, books, antiques, and so on)
● children
● pets
● friends and relatives
● holidays

The purpose of this exercise is to encourage you to be realistic about the changes in your life. If you are realistic now, you will be in a much better position to face any problems that arise later.

When two people separate, lifestyles must change in some way. To what extent they do change will depend upon the relationship between the couple, the reasons for and circumstances surrounding the separation, whether there are children involved, and the size of the family income. Recognise these changes and be realistic about how you are going to cope with them.

All the people involved in the separation may take up a fixed position that stresses their own loss and minimises the loss of others.

These fixed positions are likely to distort the real picture of how much each person has lost. There is no useful formula for deciding how much, because each item lost has to be seen in terms of what it means to that person. For example, the loss of your car may mean more to you than to someone else.

What are you going to do next?

Obviously, different people want to manage the details of their separation in different ways. Each relationship and each breakup has features that are unique—primarily the fact that it is *your* relationship and it is you going through the separation. But, at root, there is only one way to separate: **the clean break.**

'It's all right for X, she's got the house and the children.'
'It's all right for Y, he's got Z.'
'It's all right for X, she's got all his money.'
'It's all right for Y, he's got all his money.'
'It's all right for Y, he doesn't have to stay in and look after the kids, he can go and enjoy himself.'

A clean break does not mean that you separate and do not see, talk to, or have anything to do with each other. If you have children, especially, this is virtually impossible (and normally, though not inevitably, undesirable). What it does mean is that the relationship ceases to have any sexual, romantic, intimate, secretive, or emotionally positive aspects. You and your spouse should see yourselves as married in name only. You should see yourselves as the equivalent of divorced. You should focus on the *practical* aspects of the separation; how things are to be divided up and, for example, when the children should visit.

Once you have left, you might find that you keep thinking of going back. If so, perhaps you have not sorted out the problem of what you really want to do; go back to the questions listed earlier in the chapter and try to answer them again.

- Be clear about *what* you want to do.
- Work out *how* you are going to do it.
- *Do* it.

PREPARING TO SURVIVE

Surviving financially

One of the most frequent causes of anger and disagreement in separation and divorce is the problem of **money**, or, more specifically, the question of who should have how much. Whilst one partner complains of a lack of income, the other complains that the ex-partner's bills suddenly seem to have gone up. Both are probably right.

Separation almost inevitably reduces choices as to what to do with your money. Both the person leaving and the person left will be faced with the need to pay bills out of a reduced income. There is a wide range of reasons for this unhappy combination of **reduced income** and **increased expenditure**:

- Two sets of accommodation are more expensive than one.
- The person leaving may need to buy furniture and household goods.

- Accumulated debts of the couple may now need to be paid off.
- In the early stages of separation, spending often increases (especially on alcohol and entertainments).
- The person leaving may spend more on the children in order to compensate for feelings of guilt.
- Legal bills may need to be paid.

Chapters 4 and 6 give detailed advice on how to deal with some of the immediate financial problems of separation and divorce, but certain general points also apply here:

- Be realistic about the fact that your income will be less.
- Do not spend more to compensate for having less.
- Deal with any financial problems as a matter of urgency—don't let problems accumulate. List your financial priorities, and make a sensible budget.
- Don't let financial problems get in the way of managing the separation; there is probably enough guilt and anger around already without adding unnecessary money worries to your difficulties.

Surviving in your new relationship

If, having left or having been left, you have formed a new relationship, then this new relationship will need special attention. Although such a relationship is often an intensely experienced courtship, it is not like other courtships because it is subjected to many more stresses, such as:

- financial worries
- emotional problems such as guilt, uncertainty and confusion
- the feelings of your, or your new partner's children
- accommodation problems
- disapproval of others

Sometimes these stresses may make the relationship stronger because of the need to be strong together to cope with the situation. But these stresses may also highlight weaknesses, doubts, tensions, and vulnerable areas which would not affect other relationships. The new relationship needs special attention, unlike 'normal' newly-weds, for whom everyone is pleased and for whom support is in abundance. In the new relationship, many previous 'friends' may not support you—they may, in fact, be openly hostile.

For you and your new partner to survive all this hostility and stress, there are **four** key rules:

1. **Be strong and single minded**. If the relationship is what you want (go back, if necessary, to the earlier questions), then look after it. Keep it strong and you will benefit from its strength. Don't let guilt spoil it.

2. **Take one problem at a time and deal with it**. When you feel there is too much to cope with, tackle each problem separately, using the strength of your new relationship as a base. A good general does not like to fight on too many fronts, and the same should apply to the way in which you deal with your problems.

3. **Support each other**. You need each other.

4. **Be honest with each other**. The truth is an excellent foundation upon which to build a new relationship.

Survival here means more than just existence; it also has the meaning of growing and blossoming. It is pointless for your new relationship to have survived at the expense of its being able to give you anything. If your new relationship does not grow, you might, after a few months, be thinking of how to get out of this relationship. So, look after the relationship and its strength will repay you a hundredfold for all your efforts.

Protecting the children

In this area both you and your spouse have a joint responsibility to act together. You must both be able to set your children aside from your own differences. This is not to say that the children may not try to manipulate you, deceive you, take sides, or not even try to see things your way. But it does mean that, however harsh the battles between you and your spouse, you should try to fight on the same side when it comes to the welfare of the children. Try these **dos** and **don'ts**:

- **Do** co-operate on explanations—telling them what's happening, who's going where, when they can see the parent who has left, and so on.

- **Do not** complain about each other to the children. They will often see things very differently and will probably still have a loyalty to both of you.

● **Do not** necessarily put the children's interests above yours. If, for example, they refuse to acknowledge your new relationship, do not sacrifice or devalue it for their sake and do not be ashamed of it.

● **Do** recognise the conflict that they must be feeling. Though thousands of children (one in five) experience the separation of their parents, that experience is unique to each of them. It is their confusion, their conflict, and their sadness. Allow for some grief, some bewilderment, and some anger on their part. After all, think how **you** feel, even though you know what's going on.

● **Do not** underestimate children's capacity to cope. They are probably more resilient than you and can take a great deal. They can, in particular, take the truth and can work with it to arrive at their way of dealing with things.

● **Do** reassure them that you still love them. This continuity of love will provide both a background and a foundation for them to deal with the new situation.

Surviving as an individual

The final goal of a successful separation (of which divorce is only one stage) is that of *survival of the two of you as separate but whole individuals.* You should be able to operate independently of each other. You should reach a stage in which no guilt can be generated, in which each of you is **disinterested**—that is, completely neutral. Obviously, if there are children involved this may be extremely difficult, but once you have reached it, it enables you to deal with any problems much more easily.

A relationship, especially a marriage, can echo through your life, years after it has been dissolved. A separation can be like a Big Bang—an explosion of emotions which leads to a huge upheaval in your life. Its effects are felt and heard for a very long time afterwards. In a way, its echoes can always be heard if children are involved.

However, if you accept the finality of the separation and put time and effort into beginning a new life as quickly as possible, you will be able to adapt a business-like and courteous indifference to your spouse. You will no longer take each other into emotional account—and you will be that much closer to the goal of survival.

CHECKLIST

1. *Be certain* about your feelings. Ask yourself specific questions about your spouse, and, if relevant, your new partner.

2. *Be clear* about the changes that are involved in separation and divorce. These changes include financial changes, domestic changes, and relationship changes.

3. Try to *keep in control* of your situation. A marriage breakdown changes so many parts of your routine, and so many of the choices available to you, that you are likely to feel out of control. Being clear about your feelings and these changes helps you regain control.

So:
Know your feelings.
Recognise the changes.
Keep in control.

2
Coping with Your Emotions

A marital breakdown normally produces a huge eruption of emotions—an eruption which sometimes threatens to obscure your vision. What should you do? How should you react? How do you rise above it all? You may swing from certainty to doubt, from anger to guilt or from trust to suspicion.

To make matters worse, you may well have been caught unprepared for such a trauma. You will probably have to make important decisions at a time when your powers of judgement are under a great deal of pressure.

WHAT MARRIAGE BREAKDOWN MEANS

The breakdown of a marriage can be compared to the breakdown of a car. Cars break down because parts wear out, or are defective, and as a result certain processes do not work properly.

Marriages can break down for the same sorts of reasons. Parts of a marriage can wear out. They may start off as exciting, fun, new and interesting; but that excitement may wear out, leaving a boring and dull relationship. Parts of a marriage can be defective. You may find that the two of you are incompatible, that you grow apart, and that you need each other less and less. The machinery of a marriage can stop working. There is no communication, no interest in each other. The routines of the marriage, once so enthusiastically built up, have become tedious and restricting. If these problems have begun to set in, a marriage, like a car, might slowly grind to a halt—or it might suddenly explode without warning.

Running repairs
With a car, you have the following choices:

● You can mend it yourself (if you know how).

- You can take it to a mechanic to be mended.
- If things look bad, you can get rid of the car and get another one (if you can afford it).

If your marriage breaks down, similarly you have three options:

- You can mend it (if you know how).
- You can take it to a counsellor to be mended.
- If things look too bad, you can separate and find someone else (if you can afford it).

Of course, this analogy doesn't hold throughout. Cars don't have the same emotional significance, cars don't have children, and so on. But the point of the analogy is to encourage you to approach your marital breakdown in the same sort of way that you would approach your car breaking down. Ask yourself the following questions:

- What is wrong with your marriage?
- How should you respond?
- What sort of choices have you got?
- When do you have to make them?
- What are the likely consequences of your actions?

Analysing your own situation

Before you can answer these questions, you will need to analyse— to examine and understand—your situation in order to find out the important features of your separation. You will discover that using this method clarifies a very significant point. This is that your **feelings**, your emotional responses, both affect and are affected by the choices you make:

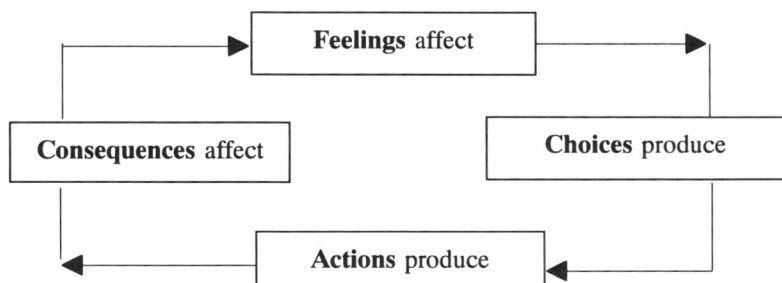

```
        ┌──────────────────────────────┐
        │      Feelings affect          │───────────┐
        └──────────────────────────────┘            │
   ┌──────────────────────┐      ┌──────────────────────────┐
   │ Consequences affect  │      │    Choices produce        │
   └──────────────────────┘      └──────────────────────────┘
        │          ┌──────────────────────────┐      │
        └──────────│     Actions produce       │──────┘
                   └──────────────────────────┘
```

Your feelings affect the way in which you make choices, affect even which choices you think you have. Your choices result in actions. You choose to do one thing rather than another, and therefore, you act in one way rather than in another. Actions have consequences, some of which are predictable, some of which are not. One of the consequences is that, now that the situation has changed (through your choice and action), your own feelings about the situation will be affected.

Feelings about:	Choices available:	Consequences:	Feelings:
Your spouse	1.	Predictable	How have
	2.	Unpredictable	they
	3.	Short-term	changed?
		Long-term	

Try completing a form similar to the one above, listing your choices and their consequences—it will help you to look at your particular situation more rationally. You may find it useful to complete similar forms for yourself, your children, your new partner or your spouse's new partner, depending on your circumstances. Once you are able to understand your feelings, you will be better placed to make the best decisions.

Improving your understanding

● Recognise the ways in which feelings affect consequences and how, in turn, consequences affect feelings.

● Acknowledge your anger, your jealousy, your grief, your guilt, your affection and your resentment.

● Try to step outside these feelings. Interview yourself as if you were playing devil's advocate. Put the other side of the question, press for honest answers, highlight the consequences of your actions, and ask if you want those to happen. Force yourself to face decisions and to be prepared for the consequences of these decisions.

● Recognise that your feelings will be a mixture of both the positive and the negative—towards your spouse and yourself. Perhaps you will like your spouse and dislike yourself; then you will want to defend yourself and criticize your spouse. You might feel a mixture of tenderness and hostility.

Case study: to leave or not to leave?

John and Sue have been married for eight years. They have two children, James aged 5 and Zoe aged 3. Though John admits that the first few years of their marriage were happy, he explains that things started to go wrong about two years ago. 'We started to argue more, often over very trivial things. It would be normally over nothing at all. Even something like which car park we should use when we went into town would lead to long silences and sulks. It's hard to believe that we used to laugh such a lot.'

John had thought of leaving about a year ago. 'It was just after Christmas. We'd had a pretty miserable few days, with the usual bickering. Jamie and Zoe obviously picked it up because they seemed to grizzle all the time. I just thought, this is it. We're not doing anybody any good staying together. For my sake, for the children's sake, and for Sue's sake, I ought to go. Just give ourselves time to sort everything out.'

Feelings about:	Choices available:	Consequences:	Feelings:
Jamie and Zoe	1. Stay for their sake	Predictable	
	2. Leave in a few years' time	They'll be happier if I stay. I won't have to explain anything to them. Their standard of living won't go down. I might lose Penny!	
	3. Leave now		I can't let not wanting to upset them now be the only thing I consider. I love Penny.
		Unpredictable	
		Will I cope? Won't they be less happy because Sue and I will keep arguing? Penny?	
		Short-term	
		Possible relief at being able to do NOTHING?	
		Long-term	
		They'll leave home anyway. Long-term without Penny?	

Fig. 1. Analysing and managing your feelings.

Feelings about:	Choices available:	Consequences:	Feelings:
Jamie and Zoe	(2) Leave in a few years' time	**Predictable** I've got to suppress how I feel now. Penny can't be expected to hang around. **Unpredictable** I don't know how I'll be able to cope. **Short-term** The children might be happy. I won't!! **Long-term** How many years is 'a few'? Will it be easier to leave in 5 years? Jamie will be 10! Zoe will be 8!	This solves nothing. I can't deny my feelings for Penny. It's not fair on anybody.

Feelings about:	Choices available:	Consequences:	Feelings:
Jamie and Zoe	③ leave now	**Predictable** I'll be with Penny (I want to be with Penny) The children will probably be confused, miserable, angry. **Unpredictable** Perhaps they'll hate me. How will I feel not being with them? **Short-term** They can come and see me. We could do things together. Will they like Penny? Will Penny like them? **Long-term** Probably be alright.	I think they could cope. I think I could. It's a question of doing it right. Being honest about how I feel. That's what's best for everybody. I realise that I want to be with Penny!

But he didn't leave. 'You just carry on, don't you? In theory it sounds all very easy. But doing it? That's another thing.'

That was before he met Penny. 'She started work at my place a few months ago. We used to speak in the corridor, nothing special just "hello, nice day" sort of thing. Then we'd have coffee together in the canteen. Then it would be lunch. Then it moved on to a drink after work. And so it just carried on. I'd tell Sue I was working late, and then go round to Penny's. That made things worse, of course. Sue got more and more ratty, so I worked more and more late.'

The truth came out in the end. 'Sue worked it out, so I admitted it. It was a bit of a relief in a way. But it does mean that something's got to happen. Sue says I've got to give Penny up. She wants us to go away for a few days. "To talk it over," she says. She thinks we can sort everything out and get back to how we were. And, as she says, "how do you explain to two little children that their Daddy is leaving them?"'

'I'm just confused,' admits John. 'When I'm with Penny it all seems straightforward. Then when I picture the kids, when I picture little Jamie with those great big eyes . . .'

John could benefit from sorting out what he wants to do. There are too many things clouding his judgement, too many things to balance against each other. He had a go at completing one of the forms, concentrating on the children.

Case study: John's decision
'It was only when I started facing up to what choices I had that things seemed to get clearer. I suppose I wanted everything. I wanted Penny. I wanted to keep the children happy, not to have to upset them. I suppose also I didn't want to upset Sue more than I had already.

'The decision to leave her just seemed to hit me. Looking at what I'd written—not just about the children but also when I did the ones on Sue and Penny—just pointed me in that direction. I knew that I wouldn't be happy staying with Sue and the kids. I only had to think back to what it had been like, with all the arguments. Leaving Sue for Penny made sense for everybody.'

Comment
Of course, someone else might have written very different things and therefore come to a very different conclusion. You should be honest with yourself when you write yours. There is no point to the exercise if you're not truthful about the way you see things.

SORTING OUT YOUR FEELINGS

Dealing with guilt

This is a feature of most marriage breakdowns, rather than something which is peculiar to you. Both the person leaving and the person left experience it to a greater or lesser degree and it is likely to influence strongly some of the decisions you make. It is, therefore, very important to be able to deal with these feelings of guilt.

It's my fault: I should have done more

Perhaps you think that your spouse has left because you were not attentive or interested enough. Perhaps you feel that your marriage has failed because you were a failure as a husband or as a wife. But, if you really want to use the language of failure, try thinking of it this way: marital breakdowns are normally the product of a joint failure. The two of you have both failed in the enterprise of living together. You have not succeeded and neither has your partner.

It is worth remembering that feeling guilty means feeling that you have done something wrong—that an action of yours has unfairly hurt or upset someone. But, in the process of your marriage, you have probably both, at times, wronged, hurt, or upset each other. All marriages contain some hurt and upset, and some of this may not have been caused unfairly.

One way of looking at your marriage is as a description of how the two of you interacted. This is how you and your spouse lived with each other—you had *this* effect and made *these* responses, your spouse had *that* effect and made *those* responses. To say that the marriage has broken down because of a catalogue of failings on your part alone ignores this pattern of interaction between the two of you. You were as you were because, at the time, you acted and you responded as you thought appropriate.

A marriage breakdown always prompts the frustrating 'What if . . . ?' questions. 'What if I'd been more loving, more understanding, more sympathetic, more interested, and less selfish . . . ?' However, the reality is that you were not and, probably, given the way the two of you interact, you would not be if you were given another chance. It went wrong in the past; now look to the present and the future. Do not let the past end up forcing a straitjacket on the present. You must deal with the separation now, not worry about how the marriage might have been.

If the two of you think that you might be able to learn from your previous mistakes, then work on that now—if necessary with the help of a counsellor. Otherwise, concentrate upon dealing with the present demands of the separation.

What about the good times?
Again, consider the reality rather than what might have been. If you have left, then, presumably, you had what were, to you, good reasons for going. Rather than trying to remember the good times of your marriage, remember the bad times:

- What about the arguments?
- What about the times when you hated being in the house?
- What about the unreasonable behaviour?
- What about the longing to get away?
- What about your reasons for wanting to leave?

A marriage cannot survive upon a memory of past good times; it is a living thing which needs the stimulation of good times *now*.

Can we try one more time?
Separation and divorce are not things to be undertaken lightly; they are far too disruptive and distressing for that. However, if separation and divorce are the most sensible choice available, then do not be afraid to proceed. For a marriage to be worth 'another chance', there has to be a *real* commitment on both sides to change, a commitment to keep the marriage going. There has to be a central regard for each other which is made up of love, affection, and consideration.

If you cannot make this commitment, be honest about it—with yourself and your spouse. Don't waste time and energy trying again; answer the questions in Chapter 1 honestly, make your decision, and act on it. If you feel that the marriage cannot be saved because the problems with it will not be solved by trying again, why should you feel guilty?

Do not confuse guilt with pity, sadness, or regret. The breakdown of a marriage is likely to be attended by all of these feelings. All of these feelings can be appropriate. Guilt, however, is *inappropriate* if it is just a general concern that things are not perfect, and that not everyone is happy. After all, the breakdown of a marriage is never likely to be a particularly pleasurable experience.

Should we try again for the children's sake?
Children are not, in themselves, normally enough to revive a marriage. Getting back together for the sake of the children has a strong emotional

appeal and is often put forward as sufficient justification for having a final attempt at saving a failing marriage.

However, remember that agreeing to stay together in order to minimise the disruption in your children's lives is a strategy which does not take into account the relationship between you and your spouse. It is like putting a sticking plaster over a large open wound; it only covers up the basic problem—it does not solve it.

Remember also that a failing marriage will diminish your capacity to be good parents. There is a lot of evidence that children suffer more from the continuation of their parents' unhappy marriage than from the temporary distress of the breakdown of the marriage. If you handle the separation properly, you will be serving your children better than if you make a mess of living together.

Case history: for the children's sake

David and Helen had been married for eight years when, after a lengthy period of arguments, David left. They had two girls, aged 6 and 4, and it was they who influenced David's decision to return:

'I used to visit as much as I could in order to try to keep as normal a life as possible for the girls. Neither Helen nor I ever talked to them about my having actually left. It was always just "Daddy's away" and "I'll be home again on Saturday."

'After three months of this, I just came back. Not because I wanted to be with Helen, but because I couldn't bear to leave the girls. The awful thing was that once I'd gone back, being at home was a real strain. The children had become too important. When they were around, it was all right because they kept us busy with things other than each other. But when they'd gone to bed, there was this embarrassment of not knowing what to do. We didn't speak much, and when we did, an argument was always just below the surface.

'After a few weeks of this, we just fell to pieces, arguing even more than before I left. In the end, I could see that the girls weren't benefiting, so I left. This time for good.'

Coping with a change in the relationship

In a marriage, the partners build up a relationship in such a way that both of them understand the rules of the game, so to speak. You share a history, a way of doing things, and the routines of daily life. The relationship is predictable in the sense that both partners know what to expect from it and know how to live it.

Then, suddenly, this complex web of familiarity and shared expectations is shattered. The marriage breaks down and, with it, the rules of your own game. Neither you nor your spouse knows what to expect or how to behave, and you will have to think through a whole new set of fundamental questions:

● How friendly should you be?
● How should you address each other?

The easy informality may have been transformed into a strained formality, as if you are stranger dealing with stranger. In a very significant way, you have become different people, not knowing how to behave with each other. Between the two of you, there may also hang a heavily emotional space. You each keep your distance but each of you is bearing what has become the burden of your previous intimacy.

Making a transition
Try to think of this strained relationship as a transition between the easy informality of your marriage and the necessarily formal relationship of separated and divorced people. As your emotions settle, as the separation becomes more definite, and your lives grow apart, there will emerge a new relationship which might be based on one of the following:

● a controlled hostility
● a measured friendliness
● a feeling of neutrality.

Feelings of grief and mourning
If a spouse or a loved one dies, most people feel the need to cope with the loss through a period of mourning. This process involves support from family, friends, and acquaintances for both the surviving spouse and any children. You probably receive a great deal of sympathy and care, and take time off work or schools. In addition, there is a description of the dead spouse in favourable terms—'he'll be missed', 'she was a lovely woman', 'you'll have some good memories', and so on. There is a **channel** through which grief can be released, including the funeral for the open expression of this grief. There is also a **status**—the widow or widower—which other people understand.

With separation and divorce, however, there is no such process (except for the legal process which is a very different matter). There is no channel for release of your grief, and no public occasion when you can express it. The sympathy surrounding the breakdown of a marriage is often expressed in terms of an attack upon the absent spouse—'you're better off without him', 'she was never any good', 'the two of you should never have married', and so on. It is a sympathy which is likely to be unwelcome and unhelpful.

A common feature of the early stages of separation is a continuing loyalty to the other spouse by the one who has been left. In the confusion of this early stage, other people's condemnation of your spouse may increase rather than diminish the unhappiness.

Perhaps it is not surprising, then, that the spouse who has been left often wishes that the leaver had, in fact, died rather than left; the proper process of grief and mourning would then have followed and the sympathy given would have stressed the virtues of the other spouse. As it is, the leaver is both lost and yet not lost to the spouse who has been left. The leaver is no longer there to give daily routines an important focus but, at the same time, he or she is, of course, still very much around. Your ex-partner may well be both tantalisingly close and frustratingly distant.

Your strategy for dealing with this grieving stage should be based upon the same method as your strategy for dealing with guilt: *analyse* and *understand*.

● Grief is a perfectly normal part of the process of separation.

● Something important has gone—something which is part of you, part of your history, part of what you were and of how people thought of you.

● If your spouse has left you, you may be grieving as much for the loss of the daily routines, and the feeling of security they provided, as much as for the loss of the spouse himself, or herself.

● Try to maintain a routine, or a pattern of your own. This will make you better equipped to cope with the implications of the separation.

● As a new routine develops, and a new normality emerges, there will be less to grieve for. Some of the things which have been lost can, step by step, be replaced.

● Grief will pass and be replaced by other feelings. Anger, for example, is likely to be next. This is not unlike the grief following bereavement in which anger surfaces—'Why did you have to die now and leave me with all this?' After separation, the spouse who has been left often experiences similar emotions—'Why did you have to go now and leave me with all this?'

Do not assume that the person leaving does so with no feeling except that he or she can now live it up, free of responsibilities, cares, and worries; this is a stereotype which is far from accurate. The leaver may also experience the need to grieve for the loss of the relationship. Even though they have decided to reject the relationship, it has been an important part of their life. They may well also miss the security and predictability of the daily routines. They may well need to adopt the same process of analysis and understanding to cope with their grief.

Whichever your position, remember, when grieving, that the daily routines of life together, no matter how comfortable they seemed, were not enough to compensate for the negative aspects of your relationship.

Coping with rapid emotional change

Clearly both of the partners involved in divorce and separation are likely to experience rapid changes of emotions, and these emotions could well be more intense than anything you have experienced before. It is a sad fact that for most people, the initial experiences of love and courtship are less profoundly felt than the wearying, obsessional anger which can surface during separation.

Be prepared, then, for both the rapid change in your emotional state and for the intensity of the experience. For example, a feeling of protectiveness or loyalty for the other spouse can change in the same day to a feeling of considerable hostility, and back again.

Denying what has happened

One response to this emotional upheaval is that of denial. The person who has been left may refuse to acknowledge the fact of the separation. This response, though unhelpful, is designed to push the world back into some sort of order—'I can't believe this is happening', 'I refuse to believe this is happening', 'You'll be home soon', and so on.

Case history: he'll be back soon

Jennifer describes the difficulties she had in accepting that her husband had left her.

'My husband left me on March 25th. I remember the day so clearly. It was such a sunny Spring day that I'd spent it doing the garden. I'd really enjoyed making it neat and tidy. After that I went inside and started to prepare dinner.

'Brian came home at 5.45 as usual, dropped his briefcase in the hall, as usual, and then came into the kitchen to say that he was just stopping to pick up some things because he was leaving me.

'I thought it was a joke at first. Just one of his jokes. So I laughed and started to tell him about the garden. All about the daffodils and the crocuses and the primroses. So he said it again.

' "I'm leaving you, Jenny. I've met someone else."

'Then he went upstairs. I followed him after a couple of minutes because I didn't know what was going on. I still thought it was a joke. He'd normally go and switch on the television to catch the news. But here he was taking his clothes out of the wardrobe and putting them into the small suitcase.

' "What are you doing?" I asked him.

' "I'm packing a few things now and I'll be back for the rest at the weekend," he said.

' "Don't be silly, darling," I said. "What's happening?"

'He closed the case and just walked out, saying, "I've told you, Jenny. I'm leaving you. There's someone else."

'Though there was a part of me that had to acknowledge that Brian wasn't there, there was another part of me that refused to accept it. He'd be back soon. It was all a silly little misunderstanding. We were so happy together.

'Even when he came back the following weekend and started to fill up the big suitcase, I offered him coffee and asked what he would like for lunch. So there he was taking shirts out of the wardrobe, shirts that I'd ironed the day before, and I was talking about lunch and shopping and the garden. Things like marriage breakdowns happened to other people, not to Brian and me.

'The next time he came for some more things, I'd begun to accept that something was happening but not that he'd left me, that our marriage was breaking down. So I started to plead with him to stop all this. I loved him, I said, and I knew he loved me.

'It was probably a good job that a few days after that, I saw Brian in his car with Veronica. There he was parked by the side of the road, his arm around her, kissing the side of her face. She was laughing.

'Veronica was sitting in my car, being kissed by my husband. I felt so jealous and angry. He'd stopped being romantic with me months before. He'd stopped being so attentive. And there she was, having that from him, that which should have been mine.

'In the space of about 30 seconds, I'd moved from refusing to accept the separation to hating Brian, to being so angry that I didn't know where to start using this anger. So I went home and smashed some porcelain figures he'd given me for Christmas.'

Jennifer's account shows not only how denial of separation can continue despite the fact of the separation, but also the way in which emotions can swing rapidly from one extreme to another during this uncertain period.

MAKING A LONG-TERM PLAN

The best way to survive your emotional upheaval is to *manage* it, and the best way to manage it is to analyse your situation, with pencil and paper.

Make a list of your emotional responses and evaluate them. Are they appropriate? Are they helping you?

- What choices do you have?—Write them down.
- Are there any other choices you have not thought of?
- What are the likely consequences of each choice?
- Which consequences are acceptable to you and which are not?
- If any consequences are unacceptable, look again at your choices.

If you are clear about what you want to do, and the direction in which you want your life to go, then keep that long-term plan firmly in mind. Remind yourself of it each day. Renew your commitment to it each day.

CHECKLIST

- Make a long-term plan and be clear about its objectives.
- Then fit everything into place, as far as possible, according to this plan.
- In this way you will find that you treat everyone, certainly in the longer term, much more considerately. Everyone will benefit, including you. You will have managed your emotions.

3
Loss and Losing

PREPARING FOR AN INEVITABLE LOSS

Until recently, the courts were expected to divide up the income and property after divorce in a way that would ensure that both sides were, as far as possible, in the same material situation as they would have been had there not been a divorce. This yardstick has been abandoned because it is unrealistic. The fact is that, after separation and divorce, some loss of income and property for each partner is inevitable. In fact, there is evidence that some couples only stay together because they do not feel able to face these material losses.

Managing feelings of guilt and resentment

You may find that guilt complicates your handling of this material loss. You will try to minimise the losses of your spouse and children by being more generous or less demanding. This attempt to soften the blow is understandable and, in a way, commendable, but it is not necessarily satisfactory in the longer term. Later, when you feel less guilty, you may want certain things back. If you are then told that you can't have them, resentment often takes over.

You may feel similar resentment if your spouse leaves and takes with them what you feel to be more than their fair share of possessions, including things which are not strictly theirs.

Resentment, as a response to loss, is powerful and long-lasting in its effects. It focuses on specific objects that one spouse wants, and that the other will not hand over.

'I never took it.'
'It broke a long time ago.'
'It was never yours in the first place.'
'It never even existed.'

This resentment then acts as a powerful barrier preventing agreement in other areas of the separation. Divorce can sometimes be compared to a battleground, and it is in this area that some of the most intensive fighting takes place. Just as some long battles have been fought over just a few feet of territory, the same thing sometimes happens with material possessions in a divorce. A long, bitter, and expensive battle can be fought over apparently minor things such as who should have a silver-plated table lighter, a set of spoons, or a photograph album.

Managing your losses

Learning how to manage and cope with loss is, therefore, of considerable importance in surviving divorce. To do this successfully, you need to deal with it not as one big problem which is beyond your control, but as a series of distinct problems, each of which needs to be approached and dealt with separately. Your response, of course, will depend on whatever it is you have lost. Answer the following questions to focus your thoughts:

1. What is it you have lost?

2. How did you lose it?

3. Do you want it back?

4. Why do you want it back?

5. Can you get it back?

6. How can you get it back?

7. When can you get it back?

8. Are you entitled to have it back?

Answer each question for each specific item you have lost. By answering these questions, you will be able to establish a specific response and strategy. If you are thinking seriously about trying to retrieve something, take into account both the time-scale and feasibility:

Time-scale
How urgent is it that you get it back? Can it wait? Should it wait? What happens if you wait?

Feasibility

How realistic is it that you will get it back? Will any cost incurred in getting it back be justified? Is it something that can be returned?

By dismantling loss into specific questions and answers, it will be possible to achieve:

- a realistic assessment of what is possible, impossible, likely and unlikely
- a set of priorities of action
- a plan of action

Above all, remember that there is no secret formula for dealing with loss. Each different form of loss will require a different response from you.

UNDERSTANDING WHAT THE CHILDREN WILL LOSE

Children can experience loss, they may be experienced as loss, and they may highlight loss. When a marriage breaks down, a family unit is shattered. The children therefore lose some things, such as the predictable routine of two parents at home. One of the parents will lose the experience of living full-time with the children, and the loss to all involved may be highlighted by one or several of the following:

- a reduced standard of living
- changes in daily routine
- the process of establishing access to the children
- new situations and relationships to be dealt with.

What have the children lost?

They have lost the day-to-day presence of one of their parents, and the security of the daily routines connected with that presence; but they have not lost one of their parents completely. The idea of a one-parent family is often very misleading. The range of parental involvement by absent parents is very considerable; some may never see their children again, others may see them at least two or three times a week. How you and they experience the loss will depend, in part, upon your relationship with them before, during, and after the separation. More specifically, then, what have they lost?

- They have lost something which is often taken for granted—having two parents living with them.
- They might have lost some income which might mean not such a good holiday, fewer outings, and so on.
- They might have lost some things that were convenient for them— someone to give them lifts, to help with their homework, to mend the bikes, to do the ironing, or whatever. All these losses are in the day-to-day category.
- They may lose contact with part of their family, such as a set of grandparents, uncles, aunts, and so on.

How should the children's losses be dealt with?

As with every problem you are likely to encounter during separation and divorce, this needs to be reduced to manageable proportions. If you talk indiscriminately about how much the children have lost, you fail to identify anything specific which can be dealt with. Try instead to look at the children's losses as a series of **situations** in which the parents are

Situation	Action
The children need help with their schoolwork.	Don't exaggerate this problem; they probably only need help from time to time. If you are the full-time parent and you were not the one who previously gave this help, then be flexible in your role. Take on the day-to-day help as required. Learn with the children if necessary. If you are the part-time parent and you previously played this role, continue with it as far as possible. Some homework is set over a period of time which can still give you the opportunity at weekends or, if appropriate, one evening a week, to help them.
Someone is needed to mend the bike, go swimming with them, entertain them, and so on.	All of these things can still be done. For both the full-time and the part-time parent, the answer is to be flexible in what you are prepared to do. Also, as far as possible, continue with your previous roles as before. Learn with the children how to mend bikes, how to cook, and so on. If necessary, try to take on some new roles, and continue with the old ones as well.

required to play certain **roles**—this applies both to the parent who has the children and to the one who does not.

Every parent is required, during the day-to-day care of children, constantly to play different roles, or to fulfil different functions. For example these functions might include feeding, dressing, bathing, taking to and collecting from school, helping with homework, entertaining, comforting, nursing, advising and disciplining.

It is surely inevitable that this process of parenting will be affected by separation and divorce, and this is usually what people mean when they talk of children's losses as the result of a divorce—'One parent cannot provide the services of two', 'A part-time parent can never be the same as a full-time parent', and so on.

However, if you are successful in identifying each situation and playing at least some of the roles as required, you will find that the quality of parenting need not be affected as badly as most people seem to think. Look at the examples on page 40.

You might find it helpful to write out your own examples and, if possible, through negotiation with your ex-partner, provide your own answers. Who will do what, and when? As you try to answer these questions, you will need to use one of two methods—either **role continuation** or **role flexibility**.

Role continuation
There are many roles that you can still play: anything from adviser, comforter, and entertainer to mender of bikes, helper with homework, baker of cakes, fashion consultant, sports coach, and so on.

Role flexibility
Some roles will need to be changed if you are no longer both with the children on a day-to-day basis. So, adjust your previous roles to the new situation. Be positive; use your time to do new things—to become a mender of bikes, a helper with homework, a baker of cakes, fashion consultant, sports coach and so on.

You will be surprised how many things you can still do and how many new things you can do for the first time.

THE LOSS OF PARENTING

Obviously there is a lot of overlap between what your children have lost and what you have lost; but the losses are in no way identical. Although your children will have lost a great deal, many of their needs will still be met—for example, your spouse may substitute for you in your absence, cooking where you once cooked, driving them about where you once drove them and so on. So you may lose more than they do; if your spouse helps them with their homework rather than you, then the children have help. They have not lost this aspect of their life. You have.

In addition, you may feel that you have lost respect, lost face, and lost status. You may feel that, because you were the one who left, you are not entitled to love them any more. You may have lost that easy, everyday relationship which you had before—a solid, central, powerful bond which comes from daily contact. So you may approach them almost timidly, feeling like a stranger trying to get to know them, and aware that they are suspicious of, or even hostile to you.

To cope with this loss, you will probably need to use the methods of role continuation and role flexibility as mentioned above. In this way, a *new* solid and powerful relationship can be built up. It may never be possible to achieve the same everyday normality that you had before the separation, but a new relationship which is still strong and dependable can be built up.

What has the full-time parent lost?

As we have seen, you may have to continue with previous roles and take on some new ones. The children will almost certainly need you much more than before. Being the parent who lives with them, you will have a much higher profile in their eyes. What you think and say and do will become central.

Your main loss, then, is the benefit of sharing the burden. Perhaps your spouse did not help much anyway but at least there was always the second viewpoint, the back-up if required, and the adult company and conversation. So now that your task is more concentrated, and your presence more dominant, you have lost some of the opportunities to switch off.

Although these losses make the job of parenting more demanding, remember that this is also a gain. You and the children can grow closer together; you can do more things together, make mistakes together, and learn together. By being more flexible in your roles and by adding new ones to your well-established ones, you can see how both their loss and your loss can be minimised.

Case study: life beyond John

In Chapter 3 we saw how John had decided to leave Sue and their two children in order to live with Penny. It was a decision that Sue found difficult to accept.

'I went to pieces. I just cried and cried. I couldn't believe that something like this had happened to me and my children. Oh, I knew all about those figures. One in three marriages end in divorce. But, as I used to say, that leaves two out of three that don't. And mine was going to be one of those two. Well, it wasn't. And I felt such a failure. My husband had gone off with another woman.

'I used to get loads of sympathy. I used to get so much that, in the end, it wasn't doing me any good. People would take Jamie and Zoe "off my hands", as they put it, so I could have a rest, "put my feet up".

'It was one of those mornings that Zoe had been taken off my hands (and Jamie was at school) that I stood in the bathroom and caught sight of myself in the mirror. I looked awful. Uncombed hair, no make-up, looking red-eyed, and pathetic. "You pathetic woman," I said. "Just look at you. What's all this about?"

'I can remember screaming at this reflection, using the most wonderfully foul lauguage. I had a good howl and then made the shift. I was Sue Goddard. I was important. And one of the ways in which I was important was that I was Jamie and Zoe's mother.

'I don't think the children knew what had hit them. From pathetic mum of the year to Supermum in a day. We did things. We went places. We had picnics by the river, we made a vegetable patch (I loved digging out John's roses), we made endless cakes and pies and biscuits.

'It was all too much, of course. We were living at a pace which we couldn't keep up. It was Jamie who pulled me back in the end. I'd met him from school and suggested a walk down to the river in order to feed the ducks. It wasn't a very nice day but Supermum didn't take a few drops of rain into account. "Can't we go home and watch telly instead?" he asked. "Watch telly?" I said, as if it was the most bizarre idea I'd ever heard.

'But then I realised. That's what people did. That's what his friends and their mums would be doing. Watching TV with a drink and a biscuit. So that's what we did. And it was wonderful just switching off, just being the three of us doing ordinary things and enjoying it.

'I've now got my act together. The kids and I still do all sorts of things together, but the pace is a bit slower. I'm not saying Jamie and Zoe don't miss John, but there's a routine back in their life. Things happen because I won't let them not happen.'

Stepchildren and stepparents ·

Depending on your circumstances, the introduction of a stepparent and stepchildren can change relationships from familiar and straightforward to strange, strained and complicated. Perhaps your ex-partner leaves you and your children to go and live with someone else and their children, or you leave your spouse and children to go and live with your new partner and their children. Different combinations abound—you may find yourself living with children for the first time, or coming to terms with a life largely devoid of children after years of parenthood.

You may find a great deal of pleasure in the
new experience of stepparenting.

The variations upon this theme involve stepbrothers and sisters, stepchildren, stepparents (both full-time and part-time), and half brothers and sisters. Suddenly, the question of who lives with whom becomes much more important.

Stepparenting is a large and complex area, and it would be misleading to try and summarise the whole subject in only one chapter, let alone one page. However, this chapter is about loss and losing, and it is worth noting that being a stepparent might have some of the following effects on your losses during a divorce:

- Stepchildren may partly compensate you for the loss of role-playing with your own children.
- A stepparent can play some of the roles previously played by a natural parent.
- Your feeling of loss may be increased if your ex-partner takes on a new partner who plays many of your roles with your children.
- Children's feelings of loss may be increased if the parent who leaves goes to live with a new partner who has children living with them.
- Your relationship with your new partner's children may complicate your relationship with your own (and vice versa).
- Your new partner's children may feel a sense of loss with regard to their absent parent.

Continuing but adapting your role

This pattern of heightened experience of loss coupled with the possibilities of compensation for loss can bring its own complications. Use the technique of role continuation and role flexibility but tailor them to fit the new situations:

1. Do not try to 'outdo' or compete with your ex-spouse's new partner; this will produce too much strain for both you and your children. You will not enjoy being with them, and they will not enjoy being with you.

2. Do not completely ignore the needs of your new stepchildren in order to please your own children; this is not fair to your partner and their own children, and will almost certainly create serious problems for everyone, including your own children.

3. Do not assume that your children will see your partner's children as compensation for their loss and vice versa.

4. Do not expect your partner's children to be substitutes for your own, and therefore a complete cure for your feelings of loss. They are different and your relationship with them, at least in the beginning, is very different.

5. On the other hand, do expect to have a great deal of pleasure being with your partner's children.

Case study: taking on Jamie and Zoe

It was some time after John left Sue and the children before Penny met them.

'I suppose I didn't want to get involved. I don't think that's necessarily a good thing, but it just seemed right at the time. John used to collect Jamie and Zoe from home and just take them out. It sounds all very familiar access stuff, I suppose: the park, the museum, McDonalds. In the end, of course, swings, roundabouts, stuffed animals, and burgers get a bit boring all round. So he asked if he could bring them back here. I said I'd love it if he did, but very much hoped he wouldn't.

'That first meeting was quite a strain. I've got a couple of nieces who seem happy enough to come and see Aunty Penny occasionally. But they haven't got any hang-ups about who I am and what I mean to them. But with Jamie and Zoe it was different. They'd obviously heard things about me. I hoped John had made sure they were nice things, although I was sure their mother had not been so charitable.

'Anyway, we got through that first meeting with the help of ice cream and a Disney video (which they'd already seen, Jamie explained). It was funny watching John trying far too hard to be nice all the time, even when Jamie pinched Zoe's nose. It was all too unnatural. That's what I didn't like. None of us was sure of what to do next.

'After that, they would come usually every other Saturday afternoon. I'd never admit it to John but I used to pray—really pray—that they wouldn't. It was just so forced. Even four or five months later, we weren't properly relaxed. Then Jamie announced that he didn't want to come any more.

'Looking back, that was a turning point. Little Zoe used to come on her own. And she and I got on like a house on fire. We'd make things together, we'd laugh at John's silly fussing, we'd do finger painting and get in a mess. I taught her to play a few notes on my old recorder—London's burning—and she taught me how to play one of these electronic games.

'But I really felt as if I was learning how to be a stepmum when, one afternoon, just as John was packing her things up to take her home, she put her arms around me and kissed me.

'Jamie still won't visit and this upsets John. But, as I've said to him, Jamie's solving his problems this way. You can't rush these things. Learning to be a stepparent isn't always easy, because you're not always sure of the rules. Children aren't either. This is why it can be such a funny business. At least Zoe seems to have got the hang of it!'

Stepfamily (The National Stepfamily Association)

If you feel you need help or guidance, you might find that **Stepfamily (The National Stepfamily Association)** is a helpful organisation. Its aim is to offer practical help, support, information, and advice to all members of stepfamilies, married or unmarried, full-time or part-time, parents and children, and to liaise with those working with stepfamilies.

An annual subscription (from £5.00 for the unwaged to £20.00 for a couple) will give you a number of useful things. There is a newsletter for adults (*Stepfamily*) and also one for children (*Stepladder*). There are discounts on the wide range of very useful publications. There is also the opportunity to join their network of self-help groups and to become a local contact for such groups.

Stepfamily also provides a telephone counselling service which gives 'confidential help in times of crisis, or stress'. Anyone can use this service—both adults and children, whether or not members of **Stepfamily**—which is available weekday afternoons and evenings. All the telephone counsellors are specially trained. The number to ring is (0171) 372 0846.

A list of local contacts and befrienders is available from the main office (see **Useful Organisations** for the address).

COPING WITH PROPERTY LOSS

Ultimately neither spouse has an automatic right to any of the assets of the marriage in that only the court has the power to decide on how the assets are to be divided. However, there are some basic principles which, under the **Married Women's Property Act**, are supposed to determine who owns what in the matrimonial home.

Joint ownership

The following items are considered as jointly owned:

- items bought jointly
- items bought out of funds in a joint bank account into which both you and your spouse have paid money
- items bought by a wife out of savings from housekeeping money
- gifts from common friends to both of you.

Single ownership

The following items are regarded as being owned by one spouse only:

- items which you owned before your marriage belong to you
- items which your spouse owned before your marriage belong to your spouse
- items which you bought out of your own money during the marriage belong to you, and those which your spouse bought out of his or her money belong to your spouse
- any gifts to you are yours; any gifts to your spouse are his or hers.

These are the principles which should apply; but there is also the principle which is not embodied in a law, a principle which, for most people, may be even more important—*possession is nine tenths of the law*. If you do not have something, how are you going to get it back?

Preparing for possession and repossession

If the item is extremely valuable, of course, solicitors and the courts are going to be interested in who owns it and, therefore, who should have it. If the item is not particularly valuable, however, the courts are not going to be interested. You will have to weigh up whether it is worth your while pursuing claims for items of property. If you are paying your own legal expenses, it is likely to cost you more to pursue certain items than to cut your losses and replace them, although this does not take into account the sense of outrage you might feel about being denied your things. Even if you have legal aid, there will obviously come a point when your solicitor will have to advise you that no more can be done to recover the smaller items on a long list of property.

Making a list

To avoid getting into a frustrating and often non-productive battle, try to approach the subject of possession in a calm, disciplined, and unemotional way. As soon as possible after the separation, make a list of *everything* that is in the matrimonial home. Go through each room with a pen and paper. If you are having to do it from memory, do it slowly, thinking your way through each room, and being as thorough as you can. Go through the garage, the garden shed, the garden itself, the loft, the attic, the cellar, the cupboards, the drawers—and anywhere else you can think of.

Actioning the list

Next, look at this list and consider how best it should be divided. Use the general principles explained above as a starting point; if the CD player was a present to you, for example, then it is yours and should go on your list. If you bought that table before your marriage, it is, without question, your table. Now ask yourself the following questions and answer them for each item on your own list and the joint list.

- Do you mind doing without that?
- Do you mind replacing that?
- Why should your spouse have it rather than you?
- Is it possible to replace it?
- What would it cost to replace it?
- Can you afford to replace it?
- Do you want to spend your money, or your new partner's money, replacing it?
- How would you feel if your spouse sold it, lost it, broke it or gave it away?
- Do you want your spouse to have it rather than your new partner?

Your answers to these questions will help you decide what to do about the property. Of course, your decisions may be affected by the needs of any children involved; but remember, try and use *reason* rather than emotion. The sentimental approach will find you in, say, two years' time, bitterly regretting the fact that you left things behind or that you let things be taken.

Claiming through the courts
Although the Married Women's Property Act does allow you to pursue claims for household goods up to three years after the decree absolute, the longer you leave it the more difficult it will be to have things returned. That washing machine which is almost new now will, you may find, have been scrapped when you actually want it back. That set of records you let your spouse take for old times' sake may have curiously disappeared when you decide that you would rather listen to them yourself.

Ownership, fairness and need
When you have been through your lists and assessed the scale of the problem, then either in conjunction with your spouse, or separately, or with your new partner, go through it to decide:

- what things indubitably belong to you
- what things indubitably belong to your spouse
- what things you wish to leave, take with you or keep for the children
- what things are jointly owned (Which should you have and which

should your spouse have? Balance them according to usefulness, need and value. Thus, for example, if s/he has the washing machine, you should have the dishwasher. If s/he has the coffee machine, you should have the fizzy drinks maker.)

● which things can be distributed according to need—such as those beds which you bought before you were married, but which the children sleep in now.

The resulting 'his and hers' lists should, therefore, reflect *ownership, fairness*, and *need*. Any other distribution is likely to provoke bitterness and anger, both of which, in turn, are likely to spill over into other aspects of the divorce.

YOUR CHANGED HOME AND STATUS

If you are leaving, or if you are required to leave, you may be lucky and move into accommodation which is generally of the same standard as that which you have just left. You may be even luckier and move into accommodation which is of a higher standard. However, most people suffer some decline in standards of accommodation, and are likely to face particular worries.

When people leave the parental home for the first time, they usually tolerate poor accommodation because of the excitement of moving into their own place. However, as they become more established, people may expect more and, therefore, may be less happy with the decline in their standard of accommodation.

Renting a place

The rather dingy bedsitter can give you a necessary breathing space and time to reflect; but it can also bring home to you what a low point you have reached. You may have lost the comforts, the convenience, and the normality of your previous home. You may have lost the use of modern conveniences that you have spent some time acquiring. There are other factors which contribute to this experience of loss:

● In order to find some temporary accommodation, you may have to 'adjust' your personal history—landlords may not be interested in someone who has just left their spouse and children.

● You may have to endure a depressing tour of estate agents only to be told that no affordable rented accommodation is available.

● You may have difficulties cooking, washing, and ironing without the proper facilities. The launderette on a winter's day can seem a very depressing place when you think of your automatic washing machine. Endless take-away meals can begin to pall when you think of your kitchen.

● You may be worrying about money. Temporary accommodation and everything that goes with it can be very expensive, especially if you already have heavy financial commitments at home.

Staying with friends

Another situation which may make you feel at a low ebb is if you move in with friends 'until you've sorted things out'. If these friends are also friends of your spouse, all sorts of conflicts can arise; you may find, instead of having called a truce, you have only shifted the battleground. Your marital disputes may well spill over into your friends' lives. Frequent and lengthy telephone calls or angry meetings on the doorstep are unlikely to encourage your hosts to want you to stay.

Try not to outstay your welcome. If you have to use your friends for temporary accommodation, make it a *very* temporary use. As soon as possible, make moves to get out. Otherwise, you may find yourself losing these friends as all of you begin to get sensitive over electricity consumption, noise, when to use the bathroom, who can cook when, where to park the car, and so on.

● Don't use friends as a temporary base except in an emergency.

● If you have to use friends, do give top priority to finding suitable accommodation of your own.

● Check the local newspapers, and put an advertisement in yourself.

COMPENSATING FOR LOSS OF A RELATIONSHIP

Taking stock: looking at the positive side

Whether you are the one leaving or the one who has been left, the loss of a familiar, predictable relationship can be devastating. Even though the two of you have grown apart, have been arguing over a long period of time, and have seen the separation coming, it can still cause a deeply-felt wrench when it happens.

You might see the search for a new relationship as an urgent task. However, having just finished one relationship, it might be appropriate to use this time to examine your own situation—a situation which, perhaps surprisingly, has a positive side as well as a negative side.

You can make your own decisions
Suddenly you're in a position where you can decide what to do. You may, of course, have children with you, but it is now up to you what your programme will be. You can make the running; you will find considerable satisfaction in being required to be in charge of your own life. It becomes *your* life again.

What will you do this weekend?
How will you get there?
Who will you go with?
Do you want to cook a meal today?
Do you want to clean the house today?
Do you want to go shopping today?
Do you want to mow the lawn or clean the car today?

Recognising that you can be in charge can lead to strength, not weakness. Do not ask 'however will I manage?', but tell yourself 'I'm determined to manage'. Out of the breakdown of a relationship in which you might have played second fiddle, you can emerge as the leader of your own orchestra.

You have cleared the air
Now that you have separated, you are at least one step removed from the pattern of daily arguments, uncertainties, and deception which may have been building up. For children, a separation, if handled openly (see Chapter 5), can give them the opportunity to get on with dealing with the new situation. A background of constant arguing does them no good and does you no good either.

So remember:

● Separate, then consolidate.
● Take stock and build up a stronger position.

Using divorced and separated clubs

There are organisations designed to help divorced and separated people, most notably:

● **The National Federation of Solo Clubs**. Founded in 1965, you can find Solo Clubs throughout the country. They are designed for all single, widowed, divorced, and separated people between the ages of 25 and 65. The Clubs meet weekly or fortnightly (the day of the week varies from club to club); services available include a holiday scheme and a Welfare Officer to help with problems. The Federation also provides a monthly magazine called *The Soloist*.

● **The National Council for the Divorced and Separated**. Formed in 1974 to continue and extend the work carried out during the previous eight years by the National Federation of Clubs for the Divorced and Separated, the National Council has branches throughout Britain and aims to have a branch in every major town. They act as social clubs, providing an opportunity for those people who have experienced similar problems, especially loneliness, to come together and help each other. The National Welfare Officer provides postal advice although the majority of branches have their own Welfare Officer. The Council also provides a magazine, *NCDS News*.

For full details on how to contact these organisations, see **Useful Organisations**.

Using introduction agencies

The purpose and quality of these organisations might not always meet your expectations, and you must make up your own mind whether you want to use this type of agency. Unlike the previous two organisations, they are going to cost you money and they are much more specifically geared to finding you a partner. The previous organisations do not exist for this purpose but, of course, as a result of attending the local club's functions, you may find a new partner.

A new partner for life? A case history
Joan's husband, Howard, left her after sixteen years of marriage. She had three children, Jenny, Vicky and Mark, all of whom rallied around her when their father left. Joan, however, found it difficult to cope and frequently called on her neighbours and relatives, crying and complaining that she could not be bothered to do anything.

Ten days after Howard left, one of Joan's neighbours gave her details of a local introduction agency. Joan went along to the agency's office and filled in the questionnaire. Three days after that, Joan found herself agreeing to meet a certain Ronald Carter at a pub in the town. He turned out to be a recent divorcé with no children of his own. Ronald was happy to listen to all Joan's troubles and concerns; he seemed a very pleasant and attentive man.

They met again the following evening and two days after that he stayed the night at her house. Having stayed that night, he continued to stay with Joan and, two weeks later, they got 'engaged'. Her new ring and the champagne toasts with his family symbolised for Joan a new beginning with Ronald, the man who had, at a stroke, solved all her problems.

Her problems with Howard, however, were increased, rather than solved, by her new relationship with Ronald. The children who had so much wanted to help in the first few days found themselves relegated to being of nuisance value—for example, when Ronald was there, they had to go to bed much earlier. Joan paid little attention to them except to demand that they behaved when Ronald was around.

After three more months, Ronald and Joan were living together. Her disillusionment, however, had started two or three weeks before this. Ronald had ceased to be the attentive and considerate man of their first few days. He was now demanding, moody, and selfish. He had no interest in the children and already the girls had switched their allegiance to Howard.

Joan, however, was fearful of enduring the breakdown of another relationship and, therefore, justified to herself and to the children the need to keep Ronald happy. 'I just couldn't go through that again,' she said.

Finding a new partner

The example of Joan highlights a number of points about compensating for the loss of one partner by taking another one:

● Do not rush into choosing another partner too soon. Marital breakdown is hard; it causes hurt, it generates anger and bitterness, it disrupts the lives of both adults and children. To rush into a new relationship which you intend as having central implications for you and your children is to invite the possibility of a repeat breakdown with all the implications that go with it. Inviting someone into your children's lives as a stepparent requires much more thought than Joan gave to it.

● The attitude 'I can't go through that again so I must stick with it' is short-sighted. Joan was not deeply enough into her relationship for its breakdown to have had more than a superficial impact upon either her or her children—in fact, the children would have welcomed it. The attitude 'any relationship is better than no relationship' seems particularly unhelpful in both the short and the long term.

● Try not to assume that choosing another partner is as urgent as, say, sorting out your finances. There is no time limit on acquiring a new spouse. The early stages of a marital breakdown are not normally a good time for the selection of a new partner for life, and a new parent for the children.

4
Helping Yourself and Accepting Help

HELPING YOURSELF FINANCIALLY

At the moment of separation, or immediately afterwards, it is difficult to see what needs to be done. However, some things will need to be arranged quickly, otherwise a lot of trouble and conflict is likely to develop. Be practical and be organised.

Controlling joint bank and building society accounts

If you have any joint accounts which can be drawn upon by either of you, it is important that you do not lose control over any funds in them after the separation.

There are two things that you can do. You could ask the bank or building society to change the procedure so that any withdrawal or instructions (for direct debit, for example) will require both signatures. That will prevent funds being taken out of your account without your knowledge, but it will also, of course, limit your control over taking funds out yourself. However, in these days of debit cards and cashpoint machines, limiting the withdrawals is more difficult.

The other approach gives you much more control. This is to close down the joint account and open separate accounts. This can be done very quickly, although some agreement on the fate of the funds in the joint accounts will be needed.

It should be remembered that the money in joint accounts is part of the total assets of the marriage. Though very small amounts are not likely to make any difference, if your spouse removes money from joint accounts or builds up debts without your knowledge, you would probably benefit from speaking to a solicitor.

Whatever you do, do it as soon as you can. Any delay might result in an embarrassingly empty account.

Controlling mortgage and rental payments

These only become a problem if you let arrears build up. After separation, there is normally much less money to spare because the same amount of money may well now have to support two homes. If the wife is left in the house, with the husband still responsible for the mortgage, she should contact the building society and ask to be kept informed of any build-up of arrears; this way, she can hopefully forestall any possession proceedings or, at the very least, get advice from a solicitor or Citizens Advice Bureau in plenty of time before such proceedings.

If the property is rented, and the tenancy is in the sole name of the husband, then he is liable for payment of the rent. If the rent is not paid, the wife can pay it and any arrears which have accrued. The landlord should then deal with the wife as if she is the tenant—this applies to the tenants of private rented property and also to council, housing associations and New Town tenants. If the husband gives money to the wife on the understanding that she pays the rent, he should check that it is being paid.

If you are in any difficulties over mortgage or rental payments, then get advice as soon as you can.

- **The local Citizens Advice Bureau** is a very useful starting point.

- **National Debtline.** This organisation gives expert advice over the telephone and will also supply a very useful self-help information pack on working out budgets and dealing with debts. It is open Mondays and Thursdays from 10.00 to 4.00, and Tuesdays and Wednesdays 2.00 to 7.00. Tel: (0121) 359 8501.

- **Shelter** can provide you with advice on every aspect of housing. The *Housing Rights Booklets* series includes one on *Mortgage Arrears* and another called *Stopping the Bailiffs* (each booklet in the series costs 50p including p&p). See the section **Useful Organisations** for further information.

Joint credit cards, store accounts and hire purchase debts

The increase in the number of people having credit cards and store accounts means that, along with the other financial complications of divorce, comes the disentangling of who owes what.

There is a key difference between the **hire purchase (HP)** debt and the other forms of credit such as the store card, for example. With HP, you do not own *the goods* until all the payments are made. With other credit arrangements, you borrow *the money* to buy the goods until you have paid off the debts. Thus, the HP finance company can claim back the goods if the account is not kept up-to-date. However, there are certain restrictions on this ability to claim back the goods:

● If at least one third of the price has been paid, the finance company must obtain a court order before it can repossess the goods. Once you, or your spouse, has paid one half of the payments, you can return the goods and owe no more. Remember that the person who signed a credit agreement continues to be responsible for paying the instalments.

Make sure you are aware of any debts that need to be paid off, so as to avoid any nasty surprises.

As with the problem of joint bank and building society accounts, credit and store accounts for which you both hold cards need to be sorted out as a matter of urgency. From the main cardholder's point of view this urgency has even greater force, in that the other cardholder could be running up large debts without the concern of having to pay them off. The best thing to do is to inform the relevant companies of the change in circumstances, and if possible return both cards. The credit organisation or store can then issue a new card for the main cardholder alone.

Paying Council Tax
The person who is liable to pay council tax on your home continues to be liable until the local council has been informed otherwise. You cannot expect the council to be sympathetic to a plea that you shouldn't pay any accumulated arrears because you left so many weeks ago. So, when one of you leaves, sort out the council tax. If the tax is paid out of a joint bank account by direct debit, you will need to sort out what to do with the direct debit instruction if you close this account. The simple advice is to let the council know what is happening.

Settling water, electricity, gas, and telephone accounts
Most people still pay for water by means of water rates. As with the council tax, you should notify the appropriate water company when one of you leaves. If you have a water meter, then you should contact the company so that the meter can be read and a settlement bill prepared.

Contact the electricity and gas companies (their address will be found on your bill) and also British Telecom (or other phone company) as soon as you separate. This will enable them to transfer accounts into your spouse's name and also to produce settlement bills.

It might be extremely irritating, and would be very unfair, to be forced to pay large amounts of arrears when you weren't consuming the electricity, gas, or phone. This would be particularly annoying if you've got your own bills to pay.

As with any other direct debit payments, you will need to deal with these when you sort out your bank accounts.

Any arrears due *before* the separation will be a matter for negotiation between you, your ex-partner, and the relevant authority. As a general principle, if your name is on the account you are responsible for any bills on that account, but this will depend on the policy of the particular authority—so find out as soon as possible.

If you think you are going to find it difficult to pay any or all of these accounts, contact the local offices as soon as possible and explain your problem; there is a leaflet entitled *How to Get Help if You Can't Pay Your Bill* available from electricity and gas companies or from Citizens Advice Bureaux.

Managing your debts

Being in debt has become a very common phenomenon, with over 2.5 million people reckoned to be heavily in debt (especially with mortgage arrears). Indeed, it has become so common that many of the banks have produced their own leaflets on debt management.

You will have seen from the specific advice above that one of the key aspects of managing debts is to be active. Don't just wait for things to happen: try to be in control as much as possible. Whatever the circumstances of your separation, whether it be amicable or hostile, it is in both of your interests to get your debts under control. There is enough to worry about during a separation without having summonses from your various creditors to add to it. Just because emotions are often making the running in your life during separation—especially during the early stages—this is not an excuse for treating debts irrationally. For your creditors it's business as usual, uncluttered by emotion. If their records show that you owe £500, you owe £500 and you have to cut through the emotional confusion in order to deal with the question of paying it. Indeed, odd as it might seem—especially if you're going through the confusion—sometimes this rational activity (getting on with ordinary things like paying bills) can be a therapeutic link with the ordinary world.

So be active in keeping a watch over your financial arrangements.

A practical checklist

● Deal with any joint accounts as a matter of urgency.
● If there are any debts which you are going to find difficulty in paying, don't just ignore them. They won't go away. Write to your various creditors explaining that you are willing to pay and what you are able to pay. Most creditors will prefer to accept a smaller repayment than have the cost of taking you to court. (Anyway, even if they did, the court will be impressed by the fact that you have already made an offer to clear the debt, and unimpressed by your creditor's unwillingness to accept it.)
● Make sure that your housing bills—mortgage or rent—are being

paid regularly. Keeping your property has the greatest priority of all.

● Seek advice if you can't cope. Speak to the CAB or people like National Debtline. **The Office of Fair Trading** can give you some helpful—and free—information on the problems of debt, including *Debt—A Survival Guide*. Write to them at PO Box 2, Central Way, Feltham TW14 0TG. Tel: (0181) 398 3405.

● Even if you have few debts, get who's paying what sorted out. The two of you can bicker all you like about who did what or who said what, but get the question of bills dealt with.

Keeping your financial lives separate

Never underestimate the importance of keeping your financial worlds separate; give this top priority if you can. Though you can't always see it at the time, whether through guilt or grief or whatever, disentangling your joint financial world will actually help you to deal with these feelings. Keeping your finances intertwined is likely to be a recipe for even greater distress and anger later.

This is not say, of course, that you shouldn't try to get agreement on who's paying for what, but to stress that you are no longer a couple. It's part of the process of 'coming to terms' for both of you. If you are parents, the wish to agree on who's paying for what might be even stronger, in that you want to preserve as much stability in your children's lives as possible. But, again, disentangling your financial lives is constructive not destructive, is considerate not spiteful.

Notifying a change of address

If you have separated and moved out, inform all those organisations with which you have financial dealings of your change of address as soon as possible. You will need to keep a careful eye on your own financial affairs, and this will be impossible without the relevant statements of account, letters from your bank, and so on.

If your new address is a very temporary one, and you are not certain where you are going to live in the longer term, you can always use the **poste restante** system. The basic idea of the scheme is that you use the head post office as your address, including the words 'poste restante', and collect your letters from there.

Income tax

Though the implications of separation for your tax position are less than they used to be (as a result of the Finance Act 1988), you need to inform the Inland Revenue of your separation. This is because, in the calculation of any allowances due to either or both of you, the Inland Revenue will need to know the date of your separation.

For those people with an 'existing obligation' as a result of a maintenance order made before 30 June 1988, the regulations will be different from those affecting people with more recent separations. If you think you are entitled to claim special relief because of such an 'existing obligation', you should sort this out with your tax office (although it is very likely that you already have!).

For those people with a more recent court order or a Child Support Agency assessment, new rules apply. If there is such an order or assessment, and the payment is made to your divorced or separated spouse for themselves or for the benefit of your children, and if your ex-spouse hasn't remarried, you can get tax relief on your maintenance. (Check that you've got each of these conditions satisfied.)

The parent who has primary responsibility for the children will be entitled to an additional personal allowance which is payable from the date of the separation to the following 5 April. This additional allowance together with the single person's allowance adds up to the amount given as the married couple's allowance. However, if it is the father who cares for the children, this allowance cannot be paid in addition to the married couple's allowance in the tax year during which the separation occurs.

There are so many detailed regulations, including exceptions and variations to the general rules, that you should make sure that you speak to your tax office about the various changes in your marital and domestic circumstances. Your tax office can give you a copy of the free leaflets IR93 *Separation, Divorce and Maintenance payments* and IR92 *A guide for one-parent families*. You would also find useful IR80 *Income Tax and Married Couples* and IR90 *A Guide to Tax Allowances and Reliefs*.

You might think of tax offices as forbidding. However, the Inland Revenue claims to operate 'The Taxpayer's Charter' which promises, amongst other things, to help you by giving information and advice, to help you to understand your rights and obligations, and to treat everyone with fairness. In return, they ask you to be honest, to give them accurate information, and to pay your tax on time!

Paying National Insurance

Married women used to be able to pay National Insurance contributions at a reduced rate. Though this 'reduced liability' concession is no longer available, those women who had opted for such 'reduced liability' have been able to continue with it. However, divorce changes everything. If you are under 60 and you have been paying at this lower rate, you will no longer be able to after your divorce. You will need to tell your employer that, from the date of your divorce, you should pay full contributions. If you are self-employed, you should arrange to pay higher contributions. In both cases you will also need to inform the Contributions Agency. See leaflet NI95 *National Insurance for divorced women* available from the Department of Social Security for greater detail. (Or phone the free enquiry service; see under 'DSS' in **Useful Organisations**.)

The need for keeping complete records

Probably more than any other time in your life, it is essential to keep a very careful record of income and expenditure in the period after the separation. Once affidavits are being sworn about who paid how much, for what, and when, it is vital to be able to substantiate your claims and, if necessary, to be able to show that your ex-partner has not got it quite right. So:

- Keep all bank statements.
- Keep all cheque stubs, making sure that each one is accurately completed.
- Keep all debit card receipts.
- Keep a record of all bills paid, with receipts.
- Keep statements of all credit accounts, showing transactions and dates.
- Keep all payslips.
- Keep a record of all voluntary maintenance paid or received, including proof of receipt.

When it comes to dealing with solicitors and the courts, you will find this careful keeping of records extremely helpful. So will your solicitor.

Do not assume that you will be able to remember everything without keeping it in writing. There are so many changes going on during a separation that you will quickly lose track of your affairs if you don't keep a careful check.

Do not take the chance of assuming that your ex-partner will be reasonable, or even honest, over financial matters; bitter battles may be ahead and the hostility and disregard for the truth may take you by surprise. If your financial records are in order, you will be that much better equipped to deal with both the battles and the hostility.

Making affidavits

Obtaining accurate information about your ex-partner's income and assets is not always easy. Written declarations taken on oath and called **affidavits** are the normal means whereby both sides disclose this information. If yours is the first affidavit—that is, you are not responding to one from your spouse—you can make an estimate of the other side's income and assets. If your spouse has already sworn an affidavit which contains information on his or her financial circumstances, then you can respond to his or her account of the circumstances in your own affidavit.

Either side can put the other **to proof** of their financial situation; in other words, you ask the other side to produce evidence in support of their statements, such as bank statements, pay slips, building society account statements, evidence of state welfare payments, and so on. If your ex-partner or his or her solicitor does not produce this information, you can apply to the registrar for your request to be made into an order. Your solicitor will be able to advise you on this.

Remember: be businesslike in your approach. Try not to let emotional concerns prevent you from acting; for example, do not let a sense of betrayal stop you informing the bank that, from now on, your financial arrangements will be very different.

ACCEPTING HELP

Counselling, conciliation and mediation

Divorce is a legal matter and so is normally handled by solicitors who advise their clients what to do, how to do it, and when to do it. This, in many ways, is the easy bit. Separation, however, is not usually handled by professionals. You may not have the benefit of expert, impartial advice. Your family and friends will probably offer advice but it will often be geared to getting the two of you back together again rather than to helping you through the separation.

There are likely to be many times during this chaotic time when you feel the need to talk to someone who isn't involved—someone who hasn't already made up their mind about you, or who isn't going to disapprove. You may feel as well that you can no longer talk constructively to your partner about matters involving the children, such as contact, for example. Fortunately, there is a wide range of services to help you.

Counselling and conciliation—your questions answered

Surely solicitors are the best people to sort out problems to do with divorce?
Solicitors can only sort out the legal aspects of separation and divorce. Their work includes giving advice on financial arrangements and on those matters involving children in which the courts are going to be interested (residence and contact). But their role does *not* include giving advice on and helping with the chaos of your personal emotions. They can only act for one side and, therefore, cannot be an impartial referee between you and your ex-partner.

There are, however, various services available which are concerned with helping you to sort out the personal conflicts that arise during and after separation, and also with helping to get you and your ex-partner to talk together.

What is the difference between counselling, conciliation and mediation?
Counselling, as the British Association for Counselling explains, 'can help people to clarify their thoughts and feelings so they can arrive at their own decisions, or even make major changes in their lives'. It covers, therefore, an enormous range of difficulties, conflicts and worries; these might include bereavement, sexual problems, vocational problems, adolescence, and so on. In the context of separation, of course, it also includes any form of marital problem, whether for couples who wish to preserve their marriage, or for those who are separating, or have separated, and wish to remain that way. Counselling can be just for you, just for your ex-partner, or for both of you.

Conciliation and **mediation** services are concerned with helping couples to try to work together to reach agreement on matters arising from separation and divorce. They are, therefore, concerned only with separating or separated couples. They require the involvement of both parties and sometimes, where appropriate, include the children in part of the discussions.

The distinction between conciliation and mediation is becoming more and more blurred. If anything, conciliation tends to be concerned with reaching agreement on the welfare of the children, whereas mediation is concerned with not only the children but also areas such as property and financial arrangements. However, the distinction is becoming less and less useful in that the term 'mediation' is the one that is being used in most settings. For example, the Government's recent discussion paper (December 1993) on proposals to change the law on divorce is entitled

Looking to the future: Mediation and the ground for divorce.
A good way of seeing the distinction between counselling on the one hand and conciliation and mediation on the other is to see that the former uses the past to deal with the present whilst the latter two use the present in order to deal with the future. In other words, the counsellor uses past experiences as a key to understanding the present whilst the mediator explores the experiences of the present in order to try to solve future problems.

In order to avoid repetition of the words, what follows uses the term 'mediation' to cover both conciliation and mediation.

Aren't mediation services really just trying to bring my ex-partner and me back together again?
No. Mediation is not to be confused with attempts by friends and relatives to bring the two of you back together again. It is not designed to produce reconciliation. It is available to help you discuss the important aspects of your separation in order, if possible, to reach agreement. Of course, reconciliation can follow mediation—it does in 3 per cent of cases—but such a result is not the aim of the mediators.

It is interesting to note that there is a drop-off rate between the filing of the petition for divorce and the granting of it. This seems to show that some people are not fully committed to separation when they file for divorce. So, though mediation is not designed to bring you back together again, it can give you a useful opportunity to examine how you both feel about your marriage.

What sort of things would mediation be concerned with?
To some extent it would depend what type of mediation you want.

Child-related mediation focuses on the needs and welfare of any children involved. In particular it looks at the issues of residence and contact. With whom should the child(ren) live? Would an arrangement work where the child(ren) spent part of the week with one parent and part with the other? What sort of contact arrangements are to be preferred? Every other weekend? One evening a week? And so on.

Comprehensive mediation, as the name suggests, looks at all the problems that arise in a couple's separation. This will include all the child-related matters detailed above as well as areas such as finance, property, and assets (including household goods).

Some mediators argue that comprehensive mediation is preferable in that child-related matters can't be properly discussed without reference to other matters. For example, a dispute over property might well get in the way of agreement over the arrangements for the children. Therefore, if property matters aren't being discussed, attempts to get agreement on residence and contact could be hindered.

So would I still need a solicitor if I use mediation?
Yes. Mediation is not designed to be a substitute for the services of a solicitor. Mediators cannot act for you, take your case to court, or advise you on your legal position.

However, they might well reduce the amount of time that your solicitor needs to spend on your case. If you can reach agreement on substantial matters such as property and the arrangements for the children, this is likely to make your solicitor's job easier (and any legal bill smaller). In addition, you will probably feel better about decisions based on discussions during mediation rather than those imposed on you after battles in court.

This sounds all very nice. But aren't there any disadvantages of using mediation?
There are some who argue that mediation has its problems. One possible problem is that one partner might feel intimidated by the other and so will agree to proposals which they don't really want. A solution to this problem is in the hands of the mediator. A skilful mediator should attempt to bring the real feelings of the weaker partner out into the open.

Another problem might be that both of you somehow feel obliged to make an agreement, even though it isn't really one that you want.

For some people, the antagonism that they feel for each other can be so strong that mediation will simply not work. It is no use pretending that a mediator can make you feel less hostile if your level of anger and bitterness is very high. For some people, fighting it out in court is the best thing.

And are there any other advantages?
As well as those advantages already considered, there are other reasons why mediation might be worthwhile. The arrangements which are negotiated in mediation are likely to be more long-lasting than those produced as a result of battles between solicitors.

Perhaps one of the biggest advantages of mediation is that it requires each of you to face up to the fact that your marriage is at an end. There is no point persisting in discussions about arrangements for the children, property, and so on if this issue hasn't been addressed.

As the recent consultation paper stresses, 'The couple are . . . required to deal face to face with questions of fault and blame and acknowledge the ending of the marriage and the responsibility for this as part of the mediation process. If the couple cannot do this, mediation will cease and the couple will be offered time and an opportunity to seek more appropriate professional help.'

It is often the case that, whilst one spouse will be clear that the marriage has ended, the other isn't. Therefore, in situations such as this, part of the mediator's role would be to help the other spouse to accept that the marriage is over.

Another important advantage, according to the consultation paper, is that mediation 'enables the couple to negotiate arrangements face to face rather than at arms length through lawyers or . . . through the courts.' In other words, meeting face to face might reduce the hostility which arises when communication between the couple takes place through solicitors' letters.

How do I get in touch with the counselling and mediation services?
A solicitor might bring up the subject of counselling or conciliation, or your doctor or minister may suggest a local organisation. Your solicitor, in particular, may have in mind something like the **Family Mediators Association**; but there are many organisations, each of which has a special contribution to make, depending on your needs and background (see **Useful Organisations** for full addresses and telephone numbers).

What national counselling and mediation services are there?

- **Relate Marriage Guidance** (the old Marriage Guidance Council) is probably the best-known service. This uses carefully selected and trained counsellors, all volunteers, of whom there are over 2300 in 400 counselling centres nationwide. You don't have to be married to use them, and they are prepared to give you as much time as you need, in one hour sessions, for you to try to deal with your problems. Unfortunately there is a waiting list for appointments but, if your problem is really urgent, it is often possible to arrange an early meeting with a counsellor. For the address and telephone number of your local counselling centre, contact the Citizens Advice Bureau, check the telephone book, or contact the Relate Marriage Guidance head office.

- **National Family Mediation (NFM)** has many affiliated local services and NFM will advise you on what is available in your area.

Alternatively, you could check with your Citizens Advice Bureau. The aim of NFM is 'to help couples involved in separation and divorce to reduce the area or intensity of conflict between them and to work towards reaching agreements, especially in disputes concerning their children.' Your solicitor may advise you to use NFM and, if so, will help you make the necessary contact. The NFM helps about 6500 families a year.

- The **Divorce Conciliation and Advisory Service** is affiliated to NFM, is based in London and is unusual in offering both a conciliation and a counselling service. The counselling service, like all other counselling services, is available to anyone at any stage in the divorce process, including after the divorce.

- The mediators of the **Family Mediators Association (FMA)** work in pairs. Each pair consists of a lawyer with at least five years experience and someone who is experienced in counselling. This combination enables mediation sessions to explore financial provision against a legal background and also to look at what sort of options are available to the couple. The FMA handles about 1500 cases each year.

- The **British Association for Counselling (BAC)** is able to provide information on counsellors within easy travelling distance of your home. Because Relate Marriage Guidance is so busy, other counsellors can often help fill the gap. All the counsellors on the BAC list are members of the Association and most can provide not only marriage guidance but also help for those suffering stress and anxiety due to marital breakdown.

- There are also some specialist counselling organisations, such as the **Jewish Family Mediation Service (JFMS)** and the **Jewish Marriage Council (JMC)**. The JFMS, based in London, aims to offer a specific service to Jewish divorced and separated people, understanding and acknowledging particular religious concerns that affect, for example, residence and contact. All the counsellors are trained. JFMS also offers a children's programme for those whose parents are in the process of divorce or separation. The JMC, based in London, Manchester and Glasgow, offers a counselling service for those who are Jewish and who have almost any problem. The clients can be married, separated, divorced, widowed, or single. They also provide an Advisory Service dealing with particular problems connected with the Jewish Religious Divorce (the Get), as well as Solo Workshops which take place in the evenings for people to talk about the experience of separation and divorce.

Won't all this counselling and mediation be just another opportunity for more arguments about the same old problems?
No. The counsellor or conciliator is there partly to act as a 'referee' to stop the sessions degenerating into just another unhelpful argument. The discussions are meant to be constructive, and attempts to reduce the sessions to another argument will be declared 'offside'.

My solicitor has talked about 'in-court conciliation'. What does that mean?
This service is provided in most courts to deal with situations in which there is a dispute as to the best arrangements for the children. It is handled by family court welfare officers at the request of the court and the aim is to try to reach agreement on the arrangements for the children. Normally, as you would expect, such 'in-court conciliation' is available only to couples who have started court proceedings. In this way, it is very different to other forms of counselling and mediation which are available at any stage of the marital breakdown.

The intention of the court welfare officer will be to get the parents to agree on the arrangements for the children. The number of sessions will vary according to how long it takes to get such agreement. If an agreement is not possible, even after adequate time for conciliation, normal court procedures involving evidence and reports are put into effect.

How many mediation sessions will we need to have?
Something like three sessions of one and a half hours per session will probably be enough for most people, but the number will vary according to the nature and sources of any disagreement.

Will I have to pay for counselling or conciliation?
This depends on your circumstances; those with very low incomes will not normally be expected to pay, but most other people will be expected to pay according to the number of sessions they have. Relate Marriage Guidance does not charge for its services but welcomes contributions towards paying for its expenses. If you are referred by a court for conciliation, the services are normally free. You should always check with the organisation concerned when you first get in touch with them.

5
Coping with
the Children

CHILDREN AND THE LAW

The way in which the arrangements for children are made has been changed substantially by the Children Act of 1989. Those of you who are familiar with the system before this Act (and might have had court orders before it came into force in October 1991) will be familiar with the old words 'custody', 'care and control' and 'access'.

The 1989 Act has swept these old terms away and replaced them with **'parental responsibility'**, **'residence'**, and **'contact'**. The Act, however, has not merely changed the words; it has also changed the way in which the relationship between parents and their children after divorce is to be seen.

Before the 1989 Act, the responsibility for children was something which the courts sought to closely define. Under the old system the court would make an order for custody, care and control, and access. Under the new system, in most cases, no formal order is made. The assumption behind this change is that the parents can work out the best arrangements for their children by agreement (if necessary through mediation), without the need for the court to make an order.

In fact, the Act prohibits the court from making an order unless making an order would contribute to the child's welfare. It is believed that limiting orders to where specific problems have arisen should reduce conflict between the parents. But it goes further than this negative effect of less conflict. It is also hoped that the Act will actually promote parental agreement and co-operation.

The Act stresses that the welfare of the child is 'the paramount consideration'. In other words, your child's welfare is the most important consideration for the court. It is not a matter of balancing your rights with those of your spouse; it is not a matter of taking sides between the two of you. The most important thing is to make decisions which best serve your child's welfare.

Preserving parental responsibility

Crucial to this change is the term 'parental responsibility'. With the end of the days of 'custody' has come the welcome acknowledgement that both parents have responsibility for their child. The term is defined as 'all the rights, duties, powers, responsibilities and authority which by law a parent of a child has in relation to a child and his property.' In other words, it is concerned with bringing the child up, caring for the child, and making decisions about the child.

If you and your partner were married to one another at the time of your child's birth (or you married at any time after the child's conception), then you each have parental responsibility for your child. If you have not married, then only the mother has parental responsibility automatically. But an unmarried father can acquire parental responsibility by applying to the court, or by agreement with the mother, or by having a 'residence' order (see below).

Keeping both parents involved

The angry disputes about who should have custody should, therefore, be a thing of the past. One of the consequences of the orders for 'sole custody' (usually for the mother) was that the parent who lost custody felt that his or her relationship with their child had lost some of its significance. There was less of an incentive to keep in touch with the child, the parent feeling excluded and aggrieved. The move in more recent years to making 'joint custody' much more the norm was a recognition of this problem. The 1989 Act's shift to largely automatic shared parental responsibility is a further and more substantial step in recognising the importance of keeping both parents involved.

When the court needs to make an order

The court will not make an order 'unless it considers that doing so would be better for the child than making no order at all'. For example, if the court has had to resolve a dispute between you and your spouse because, even after mediation, you couldn't agree on the arrangements for your child(ren), then the court is likely to make an order. The court might also decide that the child's need for stability and security would be best served by making an order. A more extreme situation would be the need to make an order if there is the possibility of one of you abducting the child.

Your questions answered

What does the court consider when making an order?

- The wishes and feelings of the child, taking into account his or her age and understanding.
- The child's physical, emotional, and educational needs.
- The likely effect of any change in the child's circumstances.
- The child's age, sex, background, and any other characteristics which the court considers relevant.
- Any harm which the child has suffered or is at risk of suffering.
- The capability of each parent (and any other relevant person) to meet the child's needs.
- The range of powers available to the court.

As you can see, the emphasis throughout is on what is best for the child. Your feelings and your wishes do not appear on the list. Those of your child, however, are at the top of the list.

How would the court know what my child's wishes and feelings are?
By asking him or her. This can be done either by the judge seeing the child in private (**in chambers**) or by the court welfare officer talking to the child. The child's age and understanding of what is involved will be taken into account but, as a general rule, the older the child, the more their views will be decisive. Be warned, however. If the court suspects that the child is saying what he or she has been told to say, then the wishes and feelings they express will be largely discounted.

Doesn't a mother stand a much better chance of having the child living with her than with the father?
With very young children, the answer must be 'yes'. The 1989 Act hasn't changed this fundamental principle. It is judged that very young children should live with their mother in that a mother is seen as best able to meet the child's needs. However, with older children this will not necessarily apply. The court will want to look at the history of your family, to see who has played the most significant role in bringing up your children, to see what sort of relationship the children have with each of you, and so on.

The requirement to look at the likely effect of any change in circumstances can also be considered here. Though divorce always brings some sort of change to a child's life, the court will want to limit the disruptive effect of this change. This means that, if a child is happily settled living with one parent, it would require very special circumstances to justify moving that child. Similarly, though there will sometimes be good reasons for splitting up brothers and sisters, the court will normally want to keep them together.

What sort of 'harm' does a court consider?
The obvious examples of 'harm' are violence and sexual abuse. One would not expect a court to make a residence order in favour of a parent with a history of violence. Nor would one expect a court to make a contact order with regard to a parent who has sexually abused his or her child (except under very strict conditions). Alcoholism is another factor that would be relevant.

How would a court decide if I am more 'capable' than my spouse of looking after our children?
There are many relevant factors for a court to consider. In essence, however, the court is concerned with the question of which of you is best able to look after the child during the week. Do you have to work full-time? If you do, who would look after the children during the day/after school/during the school holidays, and so on? Obviously, the ages of your children would be very important here, with older children having different day to day needs than young children. In addition, the capabilities of anybody—such as the children's grandparents—who would help look after your children might be considered.

As ever, of course, remember that it is the needs of your children that are the most important consideration.

What sort of orders can the court make?
There are four orders. These are known as Section 8 orders in that they are covered by this part of the Act.

● *Residence orders*
For those of you who still think in terms of 'custody' and 'care and control', the idea that a parent can have parental responsibility for a child who lives with his or her ex-spouse is an odd one. It is important to remember that, under the new system, your parental responsibility is not weakened if your ex-spouse has a residence order in his or her favour. Responsibility and residence are entirely separate concepts.

A residence order is an order to determine where the child will live. Such orders can be flexible in that both parents could have a residence order with the effect that the child spends part of the week with one parent and part with the other (or the time is divided up into weekdays/ weekends or term time/school holidays). This sort of order, of course, is likely to be an unusual one in that it requires a degree of parental co-operation which the making of an order suggests is lacking. In other words, if you can't agree to split the time up between you, how would a shared residence order work?

There will be situations in which a person who does not have parental responsibility is given a residence order. An unmarried father is an example. So too are grandparents. In such cases, parental responsibility would be given in addition to the residence order. The example of grandparents shows that more than the parents can have parental responsibility.

If you are given a residence order, there are two things that you cannot do without the permission of the court or the written consent of every other person who has parental responsibility.

The first is that you cannot change the child's surname. Thus, you cannot write to the child's school telling them that from now on your child is to be known by a different name.

The second is that you cannot remove the child from the country except for periods of less than a month. This requirement makes the business of foreign holidays much more straightforward than it used to be, in that any trips outside the country had to be approved by the non-custodial parent. Though there is no limit to the number of such short trips, if the non-residential parent feels that there are too many, then he or she could apply to the court for a prohibited steps order.

● *Contact orders*
In the Act the emphasis upon the child is very clear. A contact order is one which *allows the child* to have contact with the person specified by the order. The child might have a number of such orders, to include not only the absent parent, but also grandparents and any other people with whom the child should retain contact.

As with the old access orders, the usual order will be one for 'reasonable contact' although conditions could be attached to it if they are seen as necessary. Contact can include visiting, staying-over, and keeping in touch by phone and letter. The parent with whom the child lives is required to allow such contact to be made possible.

The first person to have an order made under the Act was an unmarried father who applied for a contact order to be able to see his 15-month-old daughter. His former girl friend, he claimed, had tried to shut him out of his daughter's life. The judge granted his application for a 'generous amount of contact'.

● *Prohibited steps orders*
These orders will be concerned with 'single issues'. For example, if no residence order has been made, there could be an order prohibiting a child's removal from the country or an order to prevent a parent from changing a child's surname.

● *Specific issue orders*
These orders could be made on their own or attached to residence and contact orders. Their purpose is to resolve a dispute about a specific aspect of the child's life. Obvious examples would be education and medical treatment. If you and your spouse can agree on residence and contact but can't agree on what sort of education your son or daughter should have, then you might have to resolve the disagreement in this way. The court, as always, would put the child's needs at the top of its list of considerations.

Is it only the parents who can apply for an order?
No. Parents have an automatic right to apply but there are other categories of people who can also apply.

Stepparents cannot apply for an order giving them parental responsibility but they can apply, jointly with their partner, for a residence order. If the residence order is given, the stepparent acquires parental responsibility for as long as the residence order is in force. This shows how parental responsibility can be acquired by a number of people and is not, therefore, limited to the parents alone.

If the stepparent is married to the child's parent, the court's permission to apply for an order is not required.

Other people who can apply without the court's permission are any of the following:

● if the child has been living with you for at least three years;
● if you have the permission of everybody who has a residence order;

- if the child is in care and you have the permission of the local authority;
- if you have the consent of everybody who has parental responsibility.

There is a third category who can apply. These, however, require the permission of the court. One notable group in this category are grandparents. Though they could apply for access under earlier legislation, their position is probably improved under the 1989 Act. The court would have to look at their application for an order under Section 8 in terms of the best interests of the child, but it is unlikely that the court would not give them permission to apply for an order. Whether they get the order is something which the court would have to consider separately. There is evidence that grandparents have made enthusiastic use of the Act.

Is it true that children themselves can apply for an order?
Yes. Included in this third category are children themselves. Of course, children can't just, on a whim, take legal action against their parents. The court would have to be satisfied that the child has 'sufficient understanding' of what such an action involves. If the court was satisfied of this, he or she could apply to receive legal aid. Given that most children's financial resources are very limited, it is almost certain that their application would be successful.

It might seem rather odd for a child to be seeking an order with regard to him or herself. In the past, we have seen the arrangements for children as something which parents fought over, not as something in which the child takes its parents to court about. Indeed, it is this aspect which has led to headlines such as 'children take absent father to court'.

What sort of situations would make a child go to court?
The child might want to establish contact with a parent who doesn't . keep it up. Of course, there are all sorts of difficulties with situations such as forcing a parent to have contact with a child, and the court, as always, would have to consider what would be the best arrangements for the child. For example, one absent father—the subject of legal action by his 11-year old son and 10-year old daughter for more contact— claimed that visiting his children for contact always produced a row, and he decided that it upset the children too much. In addition, he claimed that he could not afford to visit regularly. In another example, a 14-year old girl sought contact with her mother so that she could see

her infant sister. The mother refused to see her, and insisted that she wouldn't let her daughter see the little girl whatever the court said.

A child might also want to change his or her residence arrangements. In another example, a girl of 11 applied for an order to allow her to live with her grandparents. Her parents had separated and she did not want to live with her mother and stepfather. Though her mother opposed the application, the judge gave the girl a long-term residence order enabling her to live with her grandparents. It was the girl who had begun the process by going to see a solicitor.

In another case, a 14-year-old girl obtained a 'prohibited steps' order preventing her parents from removing her from her boy friend's family's house. Her parents had divorced but were planning to get together again. The girl's relationship with her father was not a good one, and therefore she did not want to live with her mother if her father returned.

Though the media highlight such cases as 'children divorcing their parents', it needs to be remembered that parents cannot divorce their children and that children cannot divorce their parents. For example, in the above case of the 11-year-old wanting to live with her grandparents, the parents retained parental responsibility for her, even though her grandparents also gained it.

The publicity of the Gregory Kingsley case in the US might have given people a false idea of what children can do. In this case, the 12-year-old Gregory went to court in Florida to terminate his mother's parental rights (his father had already conceded defeat) so that he could be adopted by a foster family. His mother had a history of alcoholism, drug-taking and general neglect, and she lost the case. In this case, the child effectively 'divorced' himself from his parents. The British child would have to be content with something like a residence or prohibited steps order.

However, the significance of the 1989 Act is that children can *initiate* proceedings. They can walk into a solicitor's office and start the ball rolling. Before this Act, they were part of proceedings initiated by someone else, normally their parents.

My children want to change their surname to that of my new husband. How can I do that?

As we discussed above when talking about residence orders, one of the conditions of a residence order is that you cannot change the children's surname without either the consent of the other parent or that of the court.

If there is no residence order, you have the power to change the children's surname by exercising parental responsibility. However, if your ex-husband objected, he could apply to the court for a specific issue order preventing you from making this change. Of course, by the same Act, your children could also apply for a specific issue order which would enable them to be known by your new husband's name.

In either case, the court would look at what is in the welfare of your children. In the past, courts have normally been unwilling to agree to changes of surname on the grounds that such a change would weaken the link between the natural father and his children. However, such a position has to be set against the Act's stress upon the importance of the children's wishes and feelings. If your children want to change their names, this wish can no longer be ignored.

Children and divorce in Scotland
The 1989 Children Act does not apply to Scotland. This means that the old terminology and court orders still apply there. Parents will still be concerned with custody and access, and therefore battles over who should have custody and the nature of access will still occur.

WHAT AND WHEN TO TELL THE CHILDREN

Children worry about all sorts of things but, normally, the most reassuring thing for them is the strength and dependability of their relationship with their parents. They need to know where they are with their parents so that, although their everyday world may be changing, their parents still represent strength, support and love; above all, they need to trust their parents. For this trust to be maintained, you need to try to be as honest as possible with them at all times.

There are, of course, different ways of telling children the truth. If you and your children have always been open and frank with each other, then tell them as bluntly as you think appropriate. If, however, you find it very difficult to be so open about your separation, then you may need to think more carefully about the best way of breaking the news to them. Take into account the age of the children, how many there are (the older ones can, perhaps, help to support the younger ones), and their capacity for understanding—but when the time comes, do not evade the issue. Your honesty with them is more important than all of these factors combined.

Telling the children: DOs and DON'Ts

● **Do not** say 'You know that you fall out with your friends sometimes and then you're not friends any more.' The parallel isn't there because although children may fall out with their friends, they usually soon make up. You are not planning to.

● **Do not** put off the moment when you have to tell them. The longer you leave it, the harder it will become for you and them. Tell them as much as possible, as soon as possible.

● **Do not** underestimate children's ability to cope with the truth. If they know what is happening, where everybody is and who they are with, and have some idea of the permanence of this split, then they can get on with coping. If they don't know, or even worse, have a badly distorted picture, then they can't begin to cope.

● **Do not** on the other hand, underestimate the strength of children's fantasies. A child needs to know where the absent parent is and how long it is before he or she will see them, otherwise they may create a fantasy to explain the absence. They may also continue to nurture a belief that the two of you will one day get back together, for months and even years. So if you remarry three or four years later, thinking that the child had long since learned to live with your separation, the child may react with some hostility. Contact may break down or become less successful. Tell the truth from the beginning and you will reduce the probability of these unhelpful fantasies continuing.

CONTACT AND THE ABSENT PARENT

What's in a name?
In the following discussion, the word 'contact' is used to refer to the situation in which children visit the parent who does not live with them. This parent is sometimes called the 'non-residential' parent (being the parent who doesn't have a residence order) but this seems a rather clumsy way of describing this role. We use the term 'absent parent', although even that has the weakness that it suggests you're not there. Similarly, though we use the word 'contact', we recognise that, for many of you, no contact order exists in that you have agreed arrangements with your ex-partner. The advice on how to deal with 'contact' is designed to help you, whether or not you have an order, in that it looks at many of the

questions that come up when children visit their 'absent parent'.

What is contact for?

You may feel that this question seems so obvious as to be almost insulting. The point is, you might say, for you and your children to see one another. However, ask yourself the question again: What is the purpose of you and your children seeing each other?

Answers such as 'because I'm their parent' and 'because they're my children' avoid the question. 'Because I miss them' or 'because they miss me' are better answers in that they provide you with something specific to work on. So the real aim of asking yourself the question is to make you think carefully about what you want to achieve.

● What is the exact purpose of seeing them?
● How do you best achieve this purpose?
● Where should you go?
● What should you do?
● Who are you when they come to see you? Are you their parent, friend, uncle, aunt, entertainer, or are you not sure which?

Contact time can be an opportunity for the parent and children to learn a new skill together—such as baking a cake.

1. Do you enjoy contact time? (a) yes
                                (b) sometimes
                                (c) no

2. Do you think your children enjoy   (a) yes
   contact time?   (b) sometimes
   (Answer, if appropriate,   (c) no
   for each child separately.)

If you answered (a) or (b) to question 1, go to question 3.
If you answered (a) or (b) to question 2, go to question 4.
If you answered (c) to question 1 or question 2, go to question 5.

3. What do you enjoy about it?
4. What do you think your children enjoy about it?
5. What do you want contact to achieve?
6. What does it actually achieve?
7. What don't you and your children enjoy about contact?
   What's wrong with it?

(a) too long   (g) it makes you unhappy
(b) too short   (h) it creates problems between you
(c) a different time would   and your new partner
    be better   (i) it creates problems with the
(d) not enough to do   children of your new partner
(e) too much to do   (j) one child wants to come, the other
(f) it makes the children   does not want to come
    unhappy   (k) the children do not want to come

8. What would you miss if you didn't see your children?
9. What would your children miss if they didn't see you?
10. What would you gain if you didn't see your children?
11. What would your children gain if they didn't see you?

Questions 10 and 11 are designed to encourage you to be honest
about time and how you and your children should best use it.

12. Could contact be better? How?

The last question takes us back to question 7. All the problems
identified there can be turned into strategies for change, and for
making better use of contact.

Fig. 2. Contact time—a questionnaire.

It is very easy to forget—and very important to remember—that being an absent parent and being a full-time parent are *not* the same thing. They are very different roles.

'I'm their parent and they should want to see me.' Why? The contact relationship needs to have something more than just the 'I'm the parent' aspect to it. It is not the same as living full-time with a child, because in a full-time situation, the relationship is much less in need of clear definition. The child does not have to think about this relationship because it has been built up slowly and continuously without complications.

Contact visits, however, mark the beginning of a new relationship which is uncertain for both you and the children; it may be confusing, and even embarrassing. Seeing them away from the normal home setting, and being seen by them away from home, and perhaps with another partner, is a new and sometimes difficult experience for everyone involved. Furthermore, in a 'normal' family, parents and children don't simply sit and look at each other wondering what to say or do next. The artificiality of trying to make conversation with each other and of trying to fill the slowly passing hours tends to emphasise the strange situation in which you find yourselves.

What should I do with the children during contact time?

Children often approach contact with confused expectations—'what will happen when I go?' They may expect you to continue in your previous relationship with them, but since you cannot simply take that relationship with you when you leave, they, and you, may be disappointed. You will need to play a more active role than before, initiating action so that all of you do not just become bored.

If there is nothing to do, you will be bored by them and they will be bored by you. If you plan nothing, nothing is likely to happen. This does not mean that you must always take the children out on fantastic excursions; it simply means that you should have some idea of what you are going to do with them—even if it is only staying in to watch a video or bake a cake together.

Contact time—a questionnaire

If you don't know what you want from your contact visits, then you may drift without any idea of how you want your relationship with your children to develop. Complete the questionnaire about contact on page 82 and see what your answers are telling you. Be honest about your answers.

MANAGING CONTACT TIME

If contact time is too long

The feeling that contact time is too long often has little to do with the actual amount of time you spend together. Sometimes an hour can be too long. Sometimes a weekend isn't long enough. Perhaps contact time seems too long because you've got other things you'd rather be doing—if this is the case, be honest about it. Perhaps it seems too long because neither you nor the child is enjoying it. Whatever the reason, you can adopt one of two approaches, depending on what exactly the problem is:

1. If the time drags heavily, then *plan your contact time properly*. Decide what you are going to do. Where will you go? How will you get there? If you are going to stay at home, what are you going to do? Is it enough? Do you and your child really want to do it?

2. If you've got other things you'd rather be doing, see if you can *combine the activities with contact*. Cleaning the car, cooking, decorating, shopping or whatever; wouldn't you have done these things with your children if you were living with them? Contact time doesn't necessarily have to be totally different from your previous family life.

If, after all this, you find that contact time is still too long, then be honest and negotiate to shorten it. Half a day of enjoyable contact is better for both you and your children than a whole day of clock-watching, boredom, and irritation.

If contact time is too short

If contact time really is too short, it will be of little use either to you or your children. If, for example, your ex-spouse merely drops the children off for an hour whilst s/he goes shopping, for a drink, or to the hairdresser, then you will not have enough time to do anything of value. If you only have infrequent contact, it will take some time simply for you and your children to again feel at ease with one another, and if you don't have much time, you will be unable to do even this. Negotiate for a longer time. If this does not achieve anything, consult your solicitor or use a conciliation service.

If contact is at the wrong time

The stereotype of the contact visit is the bored father with the bored

children going round the park, or to an all-too familiar museum on a
wet Sunday afternoon. It may seem to you that the time is too long, but
perhaps it is simply the wrong time. Sunday afternoon is not normally
the best time for contact in that, especially outside the summer months,
less will be open, the parks might close earlier, and so on.

Whenever the contact time is, if you feel it is wrong, try to change
it. Talk to your ex-spouse about doing it differently. Change a Sunday
afternoon for a Sunday morning, a Sunday for a Saturday, or a Saturday
for an evening after school in the week.

If your ex-spouse is unco-operative, see your solicitor or a conciliation
service. Perhaps if you refuse to have contact at the unhelpful time, you
will achieve the long-term aim of useful, productive contact. If necessary,
compromise; a Saturday here for a Sunday there, an afternoon here for
a morning there, or once every three weeks instead of two unhelpful
times a month.

There is not enough to do

Try to organise something for each session. The contact parent needs to
give some thought to what to do with the children. The list of possible
activities is enormous, but it will vary according to your particular
situation. You will need to take into account the ages of the children,
the frequency and duration of contact, the availability of transport,
facilities in your own accommodation, interests of your children and so
on. Obviously, kite flying in the park might be cheap and good fun, but
not if your 15-year-old has no interest in kite flying. As a general rule,
avoid the easy option of just switching on the television, unless you all
want to watch something of genuine mutual interest; they might as well
watch television at home and save you and themselves the trouble of
visiting.

Walking, swimming, sports, shopping (try a jumble sale!), gardening,
cooking, cycling, the cinema—that's just a beginning. Be imaginative.
What do they want to do? What do you want to do?

There is too much to do

Do the activities you are planning need more time? Perhaps you need
to reduce the range of activities or spread them over more than one
session. Alternatively, try to adjust the time available; more time now
traded in for less later, for example, or perhaps you just need more time
overall.

Negotiate with your ex-spouse. Your children will probably support
the request if they are enjoying the activity. Do not assume that contact

time, once established in a pattern, must always conform to that pattern.

Contact time creates problems between you and your new partner

Just because your new partner loves you, this does not mean that they should even like your children, let alone love them. They may not be very likeable anyway:

● They may make it clear that they don't like your new partner.
● They may be unco-operative, sullen, and complaining.
● They may be unacceptably demanding.

Your new partner may, in this case, begin to complain, with some justification. This is always difficult. You can complain about your own children as much as you like, but you probably feel that other people should not. Like most parents, you tend to defend your children against criticism—and it is only natural that you should.

However, don't let your defence become so entrenched that you allow contact visits to drive a wedge between you and your new partner. Your partner's criticisms may well be justified; perhaps your children really *are* sullen, demanding, and selfish. Be honest with yourself about them.

Make some allowances for your children's embarrassment and uncertainty, but do not make so many that you excuse every ghastly whine and whinge. If the children are behaving badly, then tell them so. You would if they lived with you full-time. You still represent some degree of authority—or at least, you should. On the other hand, if your new partner is being unacceptably critical, then at least be prepared to discuss the problem.

Contact time creates problems with your new partner's children

The source of these problems can be the same as those mentioned above; two groups of children are being thrust together, albeit only occasionally, and both groups are likely to have had a recent background of dispute, conflict, unhappiness, bewilderment, and argument.

Remember that although you and your partner have chosen each other, your respective children certainly did *not* choose each other. When the two groups of children come together, there is endless potential for jealousy, dislike and anger.

When your children come to see you, you understandably want to talk to them, to spend time with them, and to give them your time. Here is the dilemma; if you *do* give them your time, you may be regarded as ignoring your partner's children. If you *do not* give them your time, your children may be hurt and jealous. Try to arrange your contact so that such problems are minimised if they occur. Be aware of the problems and face up to them.

- Be sensitive to the tensions in the situation. They are not going to go away just because you ignore them. In fact, if you do ignore them, the relationship between you and your partner could suffer.
- Be prepared to try different activities which suit as many of the children as possible.
- Be prepared to try contact at different times.
- Be prepared to see your children away from your partner and their children, although try to use this only as a temporary measure if possible.
- Vary the patterns of contact time; have the two sets of children together on occasions, and on others have them separately.
- Consider your needs, your partner's needs, and the needs of both groups of children. Consider how best to meet all these needs, as far as possible.

If you are flexible and sensitive, the problems should, in time, melt away.

One or all of the children do not want to come

There are many reasons why a child may not want to go on a contact visit:

- **They are bored**. Perhaps the contact time is, quite simply, boring. If this is the case, it is really up to you to change things if you want them to come.

- **They have other things to do**. Children have friends who they want to see. They may have activities—parties, trips, staying with friends, hobbies and so on—which often occupy weekends. They may resent having to give up going into town with their friends in order to see you, especially if they are bored when they come. Would you have wanted to have to have visited an uncle or aunt every weekend at that age, when you could have spent that time with your friends? Teenagers, especially, may resent the time spent with you.

- **They feel guilty**. The children may feel guilty about leaving the parent they are living with to visit the absent parent. They may see this as a betrayal, or letting down the full-time parent. The full-time

parent may, unconsciously, reinforce such feelings with comments along these lines:
'Come back as quickly as you can.'
'Leave your teddy with me so I don't get lonely.'
The children may think that they are doing something that angers or upsets the parent and therefore may be reluctant to go.

● **They simply can't cope.** Different children will react to the same pressures differently. They may be having to put up with all sorts of pressures—for example, from the brother or sister who is staying behind, who might say something like, 'It's a good thing I'm staying or Mum wouldn't have anybody', and so on. All that you can really do in such circumstances is make the child who does come feel welcome, and encourage them to come again in the future. Try to remember that some children find this strange process of contact difficult, uncomfortable, or unnecessary.

● **The parents are using the child to get information about each other.** Both you and your ex-spouse may be guilty of this—asking the children questions about new partners, or money and possessions in the home, and so on. Try not to do this, no matter how curious you are—it puts an unfair pressure on the children. Similarly, some parents ask their children not to talk about certain subjects, such as a new partner, with the other parent. Many children can't cope with the burden of conspiracy, and would prefer to miss contact sessions rather than begin a round of lies and deception.

On the other hand, do not make the mistake of not talking to the child, or of not letting the child talk to you about life at home, or of life with the contact parent, if they want to. You cannot just pretend that the other parent does not exist, especially if the child is living full-time with them. That is, after all, the child's life of home, friends, school, relatives, pets and holidays; it is quite understandable that the child should want to talk about it. In fact, unless you and the child can talk about it, what else *will* you talk about?

Growing apart

For the absent parent there is the decline and loss of **shared history**. Any family living together builds up a history of shared events—a history of memories which generate humour or sadness or just a feeling of pleasure at being together—such as holidays, Christmases, birthdays, outings, decorating, garden triumphs and disasters, school plays, and so on.

When you lose this shared history, you lose a certain intimacy. There is less to talk about, less to remember, and less to take pleasure in. The children will continue to build up their own history and you will build up your own separate one, especially if you are now living with a new partner who also has children.

Thus as an absent parent, you need to recognise that you cannot expect the relationship with your children to remain unchanged. The fact that you lose the day-to-day intimacy and the shared history means that your relationship will be more distant in the future; so face the fact that, to an extent, you will grow apart. Adjust to it and your expectations of the relationship are less likely to be disappointed. Perhaps the model of a favourite uncle or aunt is a good one to adopt—someone who is a pleasure to visit, someone who has a special place in the children's life, and above all someone whom the children see regularly because they want to.

CONTACT AND THE FULL-TIME PARENT

Many of the inconveniences mentioned above for the absent parent can apply equally to the full-time parent—contact being too long, too short or at the wrong time, for example. Rigid contact arrangements can get in the way of organising your family life. Perhaps you have your own reasons for wanting to take them out all day on a Saturday or Sunday or for going away for a weekend.

Contact needs to be useful and productive for you just as much as it does for the part-time parent, so if your ex-spouse insists upon contact at a time when it is not helpful for you or the children, renegotiate it. If he or she is unco-operative, use your solicitor or a conciliation service. You should not have to spoil your weekends or those of your children just for the sake of an arrangement which might once have worked but no longer does.

What other problems with contact are you likely to face?

One or all of the children do not want to go

Some of the reasons for this have already been listed. As a full-time parent, try not to let all the onus fall on the contact parent if these problems arise; you have a part to play in making sure that contact sessions are as productive as possible for the children.

- **They are bored**. Recognise that they might have a point. Encourage them to have some ideas about what they want to do, so that they don't go expecting merely to watch television all day.

If the contact parent does not respond, perhaps you should tackle the problem yourself. Tactfully enquire whether your ex-spouse has anything planned, and if possible explain that the children would really like to do this or that.

● **They have other things to do.** Discuss with your children what sort of time they want to go instead—Saturday, Sunday, one evening after school, or whatever—and for how long. Encourage them to think of it as a flexible arrangement.

● **They feel guilty about going.** The children may feel that they are letting you down, and that because you don't get on with the other parent, neither should they. There is often a very strong 'coming together' between the full-time parent and the children after the separation; a strong bond tends to be created and contact seems to threaten this by letting in the outside. This may emphasise the children's guilt feelings.

You may have similar feelings yourself towards the question of contact. Your ex-spouse is no longer central to you and your children. You have started to build a new life together, and you may feel that this life does not need a reminder of the past.

However, whilst children should not be forced into contact if it is unsatisfactory, their guilt feelings should not disrupt the arrangements if possible. If you and your child have a good, strong relationship then they should be able to use this to build their approach to contact.

● **They just don't want to go.** Find out why. Use your knowledge of your child and your ex-spouse to decide what to do. Contact should not be imposed if it is counter-productive, and if the relationship between the child and the absent parent deteriorates as a result of it.

It might be wise to have a 'cooling off' period during which contact is suspended, so that both the absent parent and the children can sort out any dissatisfactions. Take your cues from your children on this—you understand them. Contact is not a sacred institution which cannot be criticised or varied. It is meant to be mainly for the child's benefit.

If you feel it might help, use the conciliation services. If you feel you can tackle the problem yourself, then try doing it your way. But whatever happens don't let the problems of contact drift, thinking that eventually they'll go away.

Remember that different children need and expect different things from contact depending on their age, their relationship with both of their parents, and so on; so do not be surprised, for example, if one child wants to go whilst the other does not. It may be that, at any one time, the content of the contact visits is meeting the needs of one child but not of the other.

The children always come home laden with presents

This is a familiar complaint from full-time parents—the child returns from a contact visit clutching new toys, games, clothes, and bags of sweets. The full-time parent often sees the motives behind this extravagance as very suspect.

Why does it happen?

● The absent parent often has to concentrate a large number of feelings about the child into a short visit. Buying endless presents may be a clumsy attempt to say a lot without saying anything.

● Buying lots of things may be an attempt to maintain status; the ex-spouse wants to remind the children that s/he is still a provider, and still important to the children.

● The absent parent may feel guilty about having left the children. Buying things is an attempt, albeit clumsy and ineffective, to discharge this guilt.

● Buying things is not necessarily an attempt to undermine the relationship between you and your child. It may be a naïve attempt by the other parent to 'keep a foot in the door' as far as the child's affections are concerned.

How do you feel about it?

● You may see an imbalance between the money spent on the children, and what you receive in child support—especially if your money is not being paid as it should. If your ex-spouse can afford all those toys for the children, surely you deserve some more money?

● Maybe these spending sprees contrast with long periods of silence when your ex-spouse does not seem concerned about the children. You feel that s/he only bothers about them intermittently.

● Perhaps you just feel that the relationship between the child and the extravagant parent is 'abnormal'.

How should you respond?

- The extravagance may well affect you more than the child. The children's relationship with an absent parent is very shallow, even calculating, if it is only built upon the amount of things bought on contact visits, birthdays and Christmas. How can such a relationship be maintained or developed? The children may well enjoy having all the toys, clothes, and so on but will still be able to appreciate that these do not add up to love. Don't underestimate your children and your relationship with them.

- If you think the level of child support is inadequate, or not being paid, then pursue the matter with the appropriate authority. Anger over contact extravagance is no substitute for using the proper procedure.

- Try to understand some of the motives for this extravagance. They may be inept and counter-productive but they may simply be an attempt to maintain status in the children's eyes. They are not necessarily intended to distress you or make you angry.

The other parent does not want contact

It is perfectly possible for absent parents themselves to feel dissatisfied with contact arrangements, perhaps for one of the following reasons:

- The other parent may have a very poor relationship with you and this hostility spills over into the matters concerning the children.

- The other parent may never have developed a full relationship with the children, especially if they were very young when you separated. In this case, neither parent nor child may need contact.

- Your child and the other parent may grow apart if they don't see each other very often. Contact could become an artificial relationship from which neither side benefits.

How should you deal with it?

1. Start, as always, from the position of the children. Do they want to see your ex-spouse? If the lack of interest is mutual, then accept that. Accept that neither parent nor the children need each other. Do not try to prolong something that is no longer significant.

2. If the children want contact to be established or resumed, then try to negotiate on their behalf. Offer to be flexible over the arrangements so that, if it is established or resumed, it will be of benefit; not too long, too short, and so on. But remember that even if the children want it, the other parent must also want it, otherwise it is unlikely to be of benefit.

3. Do not regard the contact relationship as something that has to be continued at all times. Contact can be established, suspended, resumed, suspended and so on. It is something that should reflect the needs of the child.

GROWING TOGETHER: CHILDREN AND THE FULL-TIME PARENT

The full-time parent needs to recognise, just as the part-time parent does, that his or her relationship with the children will change considerably. In fact, the strengthening of the bonds between the children and the full-time parent can be one of the more positive results of the trauma of separation and divorce. However, try not to expect too much of them.

Children as a substitute for the ex-spouse
Some full-time parents make the mistake of regarding the children as a substitute for the absent spouse: they begin to expect from the child the kind of support and comfort they once enjoyed from the spouse. This might also lead to jealousy and envy, especially towards the relationship with the ex-spouse.

None of this is, of course, to be encouraged; children cannot be expected to play the role of an adult in a close emotional relationship. A child is entitled to be dependent, rather than to be depended upon for constant support.

So if you are the full-time parent, try not to look to your children to provide a strong adult relationship. Remember that they *are* only children. Recognise that they will have a separate relationship with your ex-spouse, a relationship which you should accept without suspicion and jealousy.

CHILDREN AS WEAPONS IN THE FIGHT

At its worst, divorce can be seen as a series of battles, and children are either top, or very close to the top, of the list of things to fight about. In addition, the battle over children is likely to be one of the most bitter fights of the whole process. Why do people fight over the children? The answer depends; sometimes it is for the best of motives, sometimes for the worst.

- Some people fight for the children because they genuinely believe that it is in the children's interests that they do so.
- Some fight because the rest of the divorce has become so bitter and hostile that the children are simply another source of conflict.

The prize of gaining residential orders for the children is one of the major prizes to be won in the battle between divorcing parents. However, you should only pursue the prize if you genuinely believe that it is in the best interests of the children.

Above all, try to keep the question of the children's future separate from the arguments about money, the house, contents and who owns the car. This is not to say that in disputes over the children, who has what is not a matter of considerable importance. However, it is equally important to try to keep your anger and bitterness in the compartments where they started. If your ex-partner is being impossibly unco-operative about possessions—refusing to hand over possessions which you believe are yours, for example—then keep fighting that particular battle. Do not let their selfishness over possessions be your justification in the fight for the children; rather, fight the child-related battles for reasons which the children themselves could understand.

Child abduction
I'm worried that my husband will take our daughter abroad and that I'll never see her again. Are there any ways of stopping him?
Though this isn't a common problem, it's one that causes enormous distress for those affected by it. One estimate is that about 1000 children are abducted each year.

In the account of the provisions of the Children Act 1989 above, we looked at the different orders which could be made. The residence order permits a child to be taken out of the country for periods of up to one month without the need to get special consent. If your husband has a residence order and you are worried that he will take your daughter out of the country for longer than a month, then you can apply to the court for a prohibited steps order stopping him from doing this. If your husband has a contact order, the court could require the child's passport to be lodged with the court.

If you are worried that he will take your daughter out of the country before the court, in the ordinary way, has had a chance to make an appropriate order, then your solicitor can apply for an emergency order. In addition, you or your solicitor will need to contact the police. It should not be forgotten that another Act, the **Child Abduction Act** (1984), makes abduction a criminal offence.

If your child has already been taken abroad, then what you can do will depend on what country he or she has been taken to. There are some countries who, along with the UK, have agreed to work together to assist in the return of a child who has been abducted. Such countries are called 'Convention' countries (after the Conventions they have all signed). To find out which countries fall under this heading, contact your solicitor or the organisation **Reunite** which can give advice and information on all aspects of the problem.

Unfortunately, if your child has been taken to a non-Convention country, your task will be much less easy in that you are likely to have to fight the case through the courts of that country. However, in the famous case of Peter Malkin who took his son to Egypt in 1993 (Egypt was not a Convention country), Mr Malkin had substantial holdings in this country, and he was forced to return with his son or forfeit his property.

This shows that there are many ways of getting a child returned. But the best approach is to minimise the risk of abduction happening in the first place. If you think your ex-spouse might abduct your child, speak to your solicitor as soon as possible.

GRANDPARENTS AND OTHER RELATIVES

During and after the process of separation the normal structure of a family, in which all its members have a known role, rapidly collapses.

For the full-time parent, the problem of other relatives is not normally a great one. His or her side of the family will normally keep their same positions in the children's life; the grandparents will still be special people and aunts, uncles, and cousins will be seen in the same way as before.

Losing touch
However, the 'loser', the parent who does not have the children living with him or her, also loses on behalf of his or her own family. The second set of grandparents may see the children only rarely and

increasingly the relationship declines into one of birthday and Christmas presents. Aunts, uncles and cousins may have virtually nothing to do with the children. There may eventually come a point at which these relationships, previously sustained by the structure of the family, become meaningless. Even the sending of birthday and Christmas presents may have become a ritual without purpose—it may seem as if everybody is just going through the motions of being relatives.

Recognise the point at which the relationship has ceased to have significance, and don't try to prolong it. It is not fair to grandparents to try to keep them interested in children who are clearly not interested in them. It is not fair to expect children to retain particular emotions for people they almost never see, especially when the relationship is not being reinforced by your ex-spouse.

Keeping in touch

The role of grandparents has received a lot of attention recently. As described earlier, the 1989 Children Act has made it easier for them to seek to continue their relationship with their grandchildren, either through a contact order (or even a residential order).

Do remember, however, that the acid test of any arrangement for the children is always the welfare of the children themselves. The Children Act does not confer rights upon grandparents at the expense of their grandchildren. If giving a contact order for the grandparents would not be in the interests of the children (including being against their own wishes), then the court would not give such an order. Where, for example, there is a long history of hostility within the family, hostility to which the grandparents have contributed, then a contact order might serve only to continue the problem.

Keeping the battle going or helping to stop it

Some grandparents might be the source of much family bitterness with each set getting involved in—and possibly reinforcing—the battle between their children. Such grandparents do not help their grandchildren deal with their worries and confusion which are caused by their parents' separation.

On the other hand, grandparents who are prepared to offer their grandchildren a place of refuge from the troubles at home can perform a very important role.

They can provide *continuity* by showing their grandchildren that some things in their life can be depended on, that some people are not fighting, that somewhere there is a familiar routine into which they can fall.

They can provide a *listening ear*, coupled with a compassionate advice service which neither judges nor condemns.

They can offer *unhurried time*, time which is uncluttered by the anger, guilt, and preoccupation which fills the time at home.

It's an important role if it's done with the interests of the grandchildren at heart. If the grandparents are doing no more than serving their own interests, it's one which the grandchildren will be better off without.

Getting help

For those of you having difficulties with keeping in touch with your grandchildren, the organisation **LOGIC** (Love Of Grandparents In Conflict) can offer support and advice (see the section **Useful Organisations** for details).

CHECKLIST—DEALING WITH THE CHILDREN

- Be realistic about your expectations. Neither underestimate nor overestimate how children can cope.

- Consider the changing needs of the child. Always try to look at things from their point of view.

- Try not to get involved in arrangements for contact time which you feel are too rigid or restraining on family life.

- Do not necessarily always put children first. Your own welfare is also important and if you look after yourself, you'll be in a better position to help them.

6
Divorce and the Law

For the vast majority of people, one of the most daunting aspects of the whole process of separation and divorce is the legal one. For many, the prospect of long-drawn-out proceedings and huge legal bills is almost as disheartening as the marriage which these proceedings aim to dissolve. The aim of this chapter is both to give you some idea of what to expect during divorce proceedings, and to offer some tips on making the whole process a little less painful.

USING A SOLICITOR

How can I find the right one for me?

Always remember when dealing with solicitors that *you* are hiring *them:* you are the customer, and you might find some more suited to your needs than others. So if you do not already have one particular one in mind, shop around, bearing in mind the following points:

- The **Citizens Advice Bureau**, the **local library**, and the **Court offices** should all have a list of local solicitors. The list should contain information on which solicitors carry out family work. If appropriate, check also which solicitors carry out work under the **legal aid** scheme (see **legal aid**, page 122).

- Do not assume, since you used a particular solicitor to do the conveyancing when you bought your house, that s/he is the best person to handle your divorce. S/he may not take on divorce cases and might not be suitable for your particular needs anyway.

- Talk to other people who have been divorced, and ask them how their divorce was handled. Would they use the same solicitor again? What did they think of the solicitor for the other side? What sort of qualities were they looking for? What are *you* looking for? Think carefully about this before you begin your search. For example, are you looking for someone who is:

- ruthless
- hard working
- very experienced
- young
- interested in conciliation
- male
- female?

What should I expect from my solicitor?

Your solicitor should always act, and be seen to be acting, in your best interests. Of course, they should explain to you the rights of the other side, and advise you against pursuing an unwise claim or argument; but you should always be satisfied that the solicitor is bringing his or her full professional know-how to bear on your case, so that your rights will be defended as vigorously as possible. You may, of course, lose particular battles—and those losses may hurt—but if you are satisfied that your solicitor has done his or her best, that will be some consolation.

Can I change my solicitor?

If you are unhappy with the services you are getting from your solicitor for any reason, there is nothing to stop you changing to another one. Ask around again. That young energetic solicitor who has just started up his or her own practice might be just the one you need—keen, eager for business, hardworking and knowledgable. Get in touch. Always remember that you're the paying customer, and you want a service worth paying for. Even if you are on full legal aid, you are as entitled as anyone else to a good service. Find a new solicitor who will take you and ask your old solicitor to send all the papers to your new one. If you are on legal aid, speak to your new solicitor about transferring your legal aid certificate.

The Solicitors Family Law Association

Founded in 1982, this is an association of over 3000 solicitors who favour a conciliatory approach in their matrimonial cases.

It should not be assumed that all the members are equally experienced in family law. As the Association points out, admission to it 'is not a guarantee of excellence or specialisation'. However, you can assume that all of its members have a commitment to work according to the Association's **Code of Practice**.

The Code of Practice
The Code of Practice includes the following:

- the interests of the children should be the first concern;
- a family dispute should be approached as a search for fair solutions, rather than as a contest to produce a winner and a loser;
- child-related issues should be kept separate from financial issues;
- the solicitor should avoid heightening personal emotions;
- the solicitor should avoid expressing personal opinions as to the conduct of the other party;
- the solicitor should encourage full, frank, and clear disclosure of information;
- the solicitor should ensure that the client is aware of services such as mediation;
- before taking any step, such as filing a petition, the solicitor should consider informing the other party, especially if such a step might be misunderstood or be seen as hostile.

This commitment to reducing the level of hostility in family and matrimonial work does not mean that the SFLA solicitor cannot take 'immediate and decisive action' when required. As the Association stresses, 'Adherence to the Code is not a sign of weakness nor does it expose the client to disadvantage'. Furthermore, the Law Society recommends that all solicitors practising family law, whether or not members of the SFLA, should follow the Code of Practice.

Many solicitors who are not members of the Association might also practise according to the Code, but if you want to ensure that you have a solicitor who works according to the principles given above, contact the SFLA. They can provide an address list of local members, although they will not recommend individual solicitors to members of the public. They can also give you a full copy of the Code of Practice. See **Useful Organisations** for details.

Can I get a divorce without using a solicitor?

Yes, although you will need to consider very carefully whether this would be in your best interests. Although the divorce process itself, if undefended, may be straightforward, there are many aspects associated with divorce which benefit from the knowledge and experience of a solicitor—such as the grounds for divorce, the contents of affidavits, financial and property settlements.

However, for those who want to have a go, a do-it-yourself divorce kit is available. It provides a comprehensive guide to how to fill in the

Most people find a solicitor essential for helping them to get through the legal paperwork of a divorce.

necessary forms. Entitled *Divorce Self-help Pack*, it is available from branches of W H Smith.

The High Street offers another bargain route to sorting out your divorce. Woolworth's offer a 55-minute video, *A Practical Guide to Divorce* from Castle Communication.

PROVING THE GROUNDS FOR DIVORCE

You must have been married for at least one year before you can present a petition for divorce. Technically speaking, there is only one **ground** for divorce—namely that the marriage has irretrievably broken down. To show that this has happened, one or more of the five following circumstances must be proved before the court—these are sometimes referred to as grounds for divorce:

1. **One spouse has committed adultery**. In addition, however, the petitioner must state that, as a result of the adultery, he or she finds it intolerable to live with the adulterous spouse (except in Northern Ireland).

2. **One spouse has behaved unreasonably.** The definition of the term 'unreasonable' may depend on your circumstances but the law provides clarification in these terms: 'The respondent has behaved in such a way that the petitioner cannot reasonably be expected to live with the respondent'. Examples of unreasonable behaviour include violence, excessive drinking, excessive gambling or general financial irresponsibility, and a refusal to have sex.

3. **One spouse has deserted the other for a period of at least two years.** To 'desert', in this case, means simply to leave against the wishes of the remaining spouse.

4. **The husband and wife have been separated for at least two years and both spouses consent to divorce.**

5. **The husband and wife have been separated for at least five years.** In this case, the consent of the respondent is not required.

Case study: for better, for worse . . .

Kate has been married to John for four years. For the first few months of their marriage, John was very attentive and Kate was happy. However, bit by bit, things began to change: John started to insult Kate in front of other people and then fly into a rage if she complained about this when they were alone. Not long after the insults were the occasional thumps: 'nothing really serious,' Kate explains, 'but very frightening when it happens.' More recently, John has been spending less and less time at home and more and more money on drinking and betting. 'We never really had to worry too much about money,' says Kate. 'But now we never have enough to manage. I keep trying to talk to John but he won't discuss anything and just gets angry and hits me. When I've threatened divorce, he just says I couldn't get one because he hasn't been with another woman. But isn't his behaviour what's called "unreasonable"?'

Comment

Unlike adultery, which has a simple meaning applicable to everyone, what counts as 'unreasonable behaviour' is variable and undefined. The test, in theory, is what behaviour a reasonable person would find acceptable, but, of course, in practice the behaviour complained of has to be considered in the couple's own situation. For example, a husband's heavy drinking and frequent gambling may well be considered perfectly acceptable by one wife but completely unacceptable by another. For most people, violence to oneself and/or one's children is unacceptable, especially if it is frequent. Similarly, being insulted and humiliated in front of others is unacceptable. Heavy drinking, excessive gambling, a persistent refusal to have sex: all these would be on most people's lists of what counts as 'unreasonable'. In Kate's case, the behaviour has become more and more unacceptable and the combination of insults, violence, heavy drinking, and gambling would add up, to a reasonable person, to unacceptable behaviour. Certainly Kate would be in good company in that 55 per cent of divorces granted to wives are as a result of unreasonable behaviour.

The circumstances of divorce: some statistics

- For wives petitioning for divorce, the most common circumstance on which they have been granted decrees since 1973 has been that of the unreasonable behaviour of their husbands. In 1986, for the first time, over half of the decrees granted to women were in this category.

- For husbands as petitioners, the most common circumstance was the adultery of the wife, although petitions on the basis of unreasonable behaviour are increasing.

- For both husbands and wives, the number of petitions based on a separation of two years has steadily declined.

Case study: going for the divorce

When John left Sue to go and live with Penny, it was a bad time all round. Sue was alternately angry and pleading, shouting and coaxing, hating and loving. She could not believe that John would actually go. She also hated Penny for having 'stolen my husband'. John was all over the place, feeling bad about leaving the children, and sometimes feeling even worse about leaving Sue. Penny tried to support John but it wasn't always easy, especially when he kept going on about whether 'he'd done the right thing'.

However, after a few months, things seemed to settle down. A routine was established. The children would visit every other Saturday and a kind of civilised, if rather formal and distant, relationship emerged between John and Sue.

'I hadn't really thought much about divorce,' said Sue. 'It didn't seem that important to start all that. I mean, going to a solicitor and telling her all about my failed marriage, my husband running off with another woman, a *younger* woman. That wasn't my idea of fun. But then one day I changed my mind. Utterly changed my mind. It was in town I saw them. John and *her*. I was trudging around with shopping bags, with Zoe acting up, and I saw them. They were looking in a jewellers, and they were holding hands! It seems stupid doesn't it, but that did it. It just brought it home to me that my husband, *my* husband, was with someone else. Adultery. I decided there and then to divorce him for adultery and to drag her name into it. Good old-fashioned spite. So I went and made an appointment with a solicitor and put things in motion.'

GOING THROUGH THE PROCESS OF DIVORCE

If you are employing a solicitor, it will be his or her responsibility to handle all the necessary petitions and affidavits that arise during the divorce process. From time to time you may be puzzled, dismayed, or angered by aspects of the process which you do not properly understand; your solicitor, however, will be so familiar with the process that s/he may not even stop to think about some of the aspects you find puzzling— so do not be afraid to ask. Furthermore, when accusations of adultery or unreasonable behaviour appear in the stern wording of the court document, the previously informal unfriendliness between you and your ex-partner often shifts into a different gear which produces bitterness and great anger.

Divorce proceedings—your questions answered

How do I start divorce proceedings?
You can go to a solicitor, and he or she will deal with all the paperwork. Alternatively, you can go to the court and pick up all the necessary forms yourself. A series of leaflets explain all you need to know about filling in the forms. These are as follows:

- Leaflet 1: About divorce
- Leaflet 2: I want to get a divorce—what do I do?
- Leaflet 3: Children and divorce
- Leaflet 4: The respondent has replied to my petition—what must I do?
- Leaflet 5: I have a decree nisi—what must I do next?

These leaflets are written very clearly—they have been awarded the 'Crystal Mark' which shows that they have been approved by the 'Plain

English Campaign'. They take you through all the stages of the divorce, including the detail of what the forms ask you and how to answer the questions. Even if you plan to use a solicitor, these leaflets are a useful preparation for what is to come.

The court officials can advise you on what you need to do, but cannot act on your behalf. Staff of CABs can also advise you, including advising you on how to fill in the forms.

As you will see on page 125, unless your income is very low, you are not entitled to legal aid for a solicitor to prepare your divorce petition. Many of you might, therefore, be doing this part of your divorce yourself. If you are, you should be very careful that you fill in these forms as accurately and as fully as you can. Look at what the questions are asking you. Look at the examples given in the leaflets mentioned above. Look at the examples in this book. There is evidence that courts are becoming increasingly strict about the forms being filled in completely accurately. If yours has a mistake in it—even a very minor one—your petition might not go forward, leading to delays and frustration.

Once I've started divorce proceedings, can I stop them?
Yes, at any time, short of the making of the decree absolute. All you need to do is to tell your solicitor or, if you aren't using one, to tell the court. You might be surprised at the number of people who start proceedings but don't finish them. One renowned firm of solicitors, the one that handles the legal affairs of the Royal Family, says that 20 per cent of couples change their minds once they have started divorce proceedings. So, if you do have a change of heart, you'll be in rather good company!

Do I have to pay to start divorce proceedings?
Unless you are on low income, you will have to pay a fee. At the time of writing it is £40 (1994), but check with either the court or with your solicitor.

What is a petition for divorce?
This is the first stage in the divorce process. The person who is petitioning for divorce (you or your ex-partner) completes the **form of petition** usually with the help of a solicitor. The form requires details of you and your spouse: names, addresses, occupations, and the names and dates of birth of any children. In addition, the petition will detail which of the five circumstances is being used to show that the marriage has irretrievably broken down (see **grounds for divorce** above).

Who is the respondent?
The spouse who is not the petitioner. It is up to this spouse to *respond* to the petition.

Who is the co-respondent?
In petitions in which adultery is given as a circumstance to prove the ground for divorce, the co-respondent is the person with whom the respondent is alleged to have committed adultery.

What is the prayer?
The formal language of the petition is illustrated by the section on the last page. The petitioner 'prays' that the marriage be dissolved. In other words, the petitioner *asks* that it be dissolved.

The petitioner is also likely to ask for several other things—for example, that the respondent pay the costs, and that the petitioner be given a long list of financial provisions. It will probably be a considerable set of demands altogether. One of the reasons for this is that the petitioner is leaving his or her options fully open by not deleting any of the demands on the printed form. This does not mean that the petitioner is likely to get all of the things asked for or even that the petitioner will actually pursue all of them. It is, in many cases, a technical consideration; if you don't ask for things now, it might be very difficult to ask for them in the future, even though, at the moment, you might have no intention of asking for them.

What do I do if I am served with a petition?
As the respondent, you will receive not only the petition, but also an **acknowledgement of service form**. A co-respondent will receive the same. This might be a good time to contact your solicitor, so that you can be certain of your position, and the solicitor can be prepared for full involvement in any subsequent proceedings.

In any case, the Acknowledgement of Service Form must be completed and returned to the court within eight days. The form contains questions about your responses to the costs requests made by the petitioner. You will also be asked if you intend to defend the divorce. Most people do not because they are happy for the divorce to go through and, anyway, defending a divorce is an extremely expensive business. However, you might object to some of the details given in support of the fact—for example, details of supposedly 'unreasonable' behaviour. Discuss these objections with your solicitor and, if possible, your spouse and try to compromise if you don't object to the divorce itself.

In the

* Delete as appropriate

KINGSWOOD County Court*

No.

~~In the Divorce Registry*~~

Between

SUSAN FIONA HUGHES Petitioner

and

JOHN WILLIAM HUGHES Respondent

Divorce Petition

Full name and address of the petitioner or of solicitors if they are acting for the petitioner.

Printed in the UK for HMSO 2/94 Dd 8423838 C950 38806 G6783

Fig. 3. A petition for divorce (this and the following pages). Reproduced by kind permission of the Solicitor's Law Stationery Society Ltd.

Before completing this form, read carefully the attached **Notes for Guidance.**

In the   KINGSWOOD   **County Court***   * Delete as
                                                                                         appropriate

In the Divorce Registry*   **No.**   94 D621

(1)   On the   20th   day of   AUGUST   19 86   the petitioner

                 SUSAN FIONA HUGHES   was lawfully married to

                 JOHN WILLIAM HUGHES   (hereinafter called "the

respondent") at   ST MARY'S CHURCH, IN THE PARISH OF NEWTOWN
                   IN THE COUNTY OF WESTSHIRE

(2)   The petitioner and respondent last lived together as husband and wife at
                   42 AMUNDSEN WAY, NEWTOWN, WESTSHIRE, WX4 9QR

(3)   The petitioner is domiciled in England and Wales, and is by occupation a
           SECRETARY and resides at   42 AMUNDSEN WAY, NEWTOWN WX4 9QR
                                            and the respondent
is by occupation a   CLERICAL OFFICER
                   and resides at   19 SCOTT STREET, NEWTOWN, WESTSHIRE WX3 2EJ

(4)   There are no children of the family now living *except*
           JAMES HARRY HUGHES born on 3rd September 1989
           ZOE JESSICA HUGHES born on 5th June 1991

(5)   No other child, now living, has been born to the petitioner/r̶e̶s̶p̶o̶n̶d̶e̶n̶t̶ during the marriage (so
far as is known to the petitioner) ̶e̶x̶c̶e̶p̶t̶XXX

108

(6)   There are or have been no other proceedings in any court in England and Wales or elsewhere with reference to the marriage (or to any child of the family) or between the petitioner and respondent with reference to any property of either or both of them except xxxxx

(7)   There are or have been no proceedings in the Child Support Agency with reference to the maintenance of any child of the family *except*

> APPLICATION TO THE CHILD SUPPORT AGENCY SENT 7TH NOVEMBER 1994.
> NO ASSESSMENT YET MADE.

(8)   There are no proceedings continuing in any country outside England or Wales which are in respect of the marriage or are capable of affecting its validity or subsistence except xxxxx

(9)   (This paragraph should be completed only if the petition is based on five years' separation.) No agreement or arrangement has been made or is proposed to be made between the parties for the support of the petitioner/respondent (and any child of the family) *except*

(10) The said marriage has broken down irretrievably.

(11)   THE RESPONDENT HAS COMMITTED ADULTERY WITH PENELOPE JANE BRIGHT
           (CALLED THE CO-RESPONDENT) AND THE PETITIONER FINDS IT
           INTOLERABLE TO LIVE WITH THE RESPONDENT.

(12) **Particulars**   ON VARIOUS DATES AT 19 SCOTT STREET, NEWTOWN, WESTSHIRE WX3 2EJ
                     THE RESPONDENT HAS COMMITTED ADULTERY WITH THE CO-RESPONDENT.

Prayer

The petitioner therefore prays

(1) The suit

That the said marriage be dissolved

(2) Costs

That the   RESPONDENT AND CO-RESPONDENT   may be ordered to pay the costs of this suit

(3) Ancillary relief

That the petitioner may be granted the following ancillary relief:

(a) an order for maintenance pending suit

a periodical payments order

a secured provision order

a lump sum order

a property adjustment order

(b) **For the children**

a periodical payments order

a secured provision order

a lump sum order

a property adjustment order

Signed   [INSERT SIGNATURE]

The names and addresses of the persons to be served with this petition are:—

Respondent:—   JOHN WILLIAM HUGHES, 19 SCOTT STREET, NEWTOWN, WESTSHIRE WX3 2EJ

Co-Respondent (adultery case only):—   PENELOPE JANE BRIGHT, 19 SCOTT STREET, NEWTOWN, WESTSHIRE WX3 2EJ

The Petitioner's address for service is:— 42 AMUNDSEN WAY, NEWTOWN, WESTSHIRE WX4 9QR

Dated this   21ST   day of   NOVEMBER   19 94

Address all communications for the court to: The Chief Clerk, County Court,

The Court }   JUDICIAL HOUSE, CENTRE ROAD, NEWTOWN WX1 1AD.
office at }

is open from 10 a.m. to 4 p.m. (4.30 p.m. at the Principal Registry of the Family Division - Somerset House) on Mondays to Fridays.

Statement of Arrangements for Children

In the	KINGSWOOD	County Court
Petitioner	SUSAN FIONA HUGHES	
Respondent	JOHN WILLIAM.HUGHES	

	No. of matter *(always quote this)*	94 D261

To the Petitioner

You must complete this form

If you or the respondent have any children
- under 16
- or over 16 but under 18 if they are at school or college or are training for a trade, profession or vocation.

Please use black ink.
Please complete Parts I, II and III.

Before you issue a petition for divorce try to reach agreement with your husband/wife over the proposals for the children's future. There is space for him/her to sign at the end of this form if agreement is reached.

If your husband/wife does not agree with the proposals he/she will have an opportunity at a later stage to state why he/she does not agree and will be able to make his/her own proposals.

You should take or send the completed form, signed by you (and, if agreement is reached, by your husband/wife) together with a copy to the court when you issue your petition.

Please refer to the explanatory notes issued regarding completion of the prayer of the petition if you are asking the court to make any order regarding the children.

The Court will only make an order if it considers that an order will be better for the child(ren) than no order.

If you wish to apply for any of the orders which may be available to you under Part I or II of the Children Act 1989 you are advised to see a solicitor.

You should obtain legal advice from a solicitor or, alternatively, from an advice agency. The Law Society administers a national panel of solicitors to represent children and other parties involved in proceedings relating to children. Addresses of solicitors (including panel members) and advice agencies can be obtained from the Yellow Pages and the Solicitors Regional Directory which can be found at Citizens Advice Bureaux, Law Centres and any local library.

To the Respondent

The petitioner has completed Part I, II and III of this form
which will be sent to the Court at the same time that the divorce petition is filed.

Please read all parts of the form carefully.

If you agree with the arrangements and proposals for the children you should sign Part IV of the form.
Please use black ink. You should return the form to the petitioner, or his/her solicitor.

If you do not agree with all or some of the arrangements or proposals you will be given the opportunity of saying so when the divorce petition is served on you.

D8A   F. P. Rule 2.2(2) (Form M4)

Fig. 4. Statement of Arrangements for Children.

Part I - Details of the children

Please read the instructions for boxes 1, 2 and 3 before you complete this section

1. Children of both parties *(Give details only of any children born to you and the Respondent or adopted by you both)*

	Forenames	Surname	Date of birth
(i)	JAMES HARRY	HUGHES	3rd SEPTEMBER 1989
(ii)	ZOE JESSICA	HUGHES	5th JUNE 1991
(iii)			
(iv)			
(v)			

2. Other children of the family *(Give details of any other children treated by both of you as children of the family : for example your own or the Respondent's)*

	Forenames	Surname	Date of birth	Relationship to Yourself	Respondent
(i)					
(ii)					
(iii)					
(iv)					
(v)					

3. Other children who are not children of the family *(Give details of any children born to you or the Respondent that have not been treated as children of the family or adopted by you both)*

	Forenames	Surname	Date of birth
(i)			
(ii)			
(iii)			
(iv)			
(v)			

2

112

Part II - Arrangements for the children of the family

This part of the form must be completed. Give details for each child if arrangements are different.
(If necessary, continue on another sheet and attach it to this form)

| 4. | Home details | (please tick the appropriate boxes) |

(a) The addresses at which the children now live

42 AMUNDSEN WAY, NEWTOWN, WESTSHIRE WX4 9QR

(b) Give details of the number of living rooms, bedrooms, etc. at the addresses in (a)

LIVING ROOM, DINING ROOM, KITCHEN, THREE BEDROOMS, BATHROOM AND TOILET.

(c) Is the house rented or owned and by whom?

OWNED JOINTLY BY PETITIONER AND RESPONDENT.

Is the rent or any mortgage being regularly paid

☐ No   ☒ Yes

(d) Give the names of all other persons living with the children including your husband/wife if he/she lives there. State their relationship to the children.

SUSAN FIONA HUGHES (MOTHER)

(e) Will there be any change in these arrangements?

☒ No   ☐ Yes (please give details)

3

5. Education and training details *(please tick the appropriate boxes)*

(a) Give the names of the school, college or place of training attended by each child.

JAMES HARRY HUGHES - NEWTOWN PRIMARY SCHOOL, SCHOLAR CLOSE, NEWTOWN.

(b) Do the children have any special educational needs?

[X] No   [ ] Yes *(please give details)*

(c) Is the school, college or place of training, fee-paying?

[X] No   [ ] Yes *(please give details of how much the fees are per term / year)*

Are fees being regularly paid?

[X] No   [ ] Yes *(please give details)*

(d) Will there be any change in these arrangements?

[X] No   [ ] Yes *(please give details)*

4

114

6. Childcare details *(please tick the appropriate boxes)*

(a) Which parent looks after the children from day to day? If responsibility is shared, please give details

MOTHER

(b) Does that parent go out to work?

[X] No [ ] Yes *(please give details of his/her hours of work)*

(c) Does someone look after the children when the parent is not there?

[ ] No [x] Yes *(please give details)*

SOMETIMES THE GRANDPARENTS, MR & MRS HASKINS.

(d) Who looks after the children during school holidays

MOTHER

(e) Will there be any change in these arrangements?

[x] No [ ] Yes *(please give details)*

7. Maintenance *(please tick the appropriate boxes)*

(a) Does your husband/wife pay towards the upkeep of the children? If there is another source of maintenance, please specify.

[ ] No [X] Yes *(please give details of how much)*

(b) Is the payment made under a court order?

[X] No [ ] Yes *(please give details, including the name of the court and case number)*

(c) Has maintenance for the children been agreed?

[X] No [ ] Yes

If not, will you be applying for a maintenance order for the children?

[x] No [ ] Yes *(please give details)*

5

115

8. Details for contact with the children   *(please tick the appropriate boxes)*

(a) Do the children see your husband/wife?

☐ No   ☒ Yes *(please give details of how often and where)*

EVERY OTHER SATURDAY.

(b) Do the children ever stay with you husband/wife?

☒ No   ☐ Yes *(please give details of how much)*

(c) Will there be any change to these arrangements?

Please give details of the proposed arrangements for contact and residence.

☒ No   ☐ Yes *((please give details of how much)*

THE CHILDREN WILL CONTINUE TO LIVE WITH THEIR MOTHER WITH THE PRESENT AMOUNT OF CONTACT WITH THE FATHER CONTINUING.

6

9. **Details of health** *(please tick the appropriate boxes)*

(a) Are the children generally in good health?

☐ No   ☒ Yes   *(please give details of any serious disability or chronic illness)*

(b) Do the children have any special health needs?

☒ No   ☐ Yes   *(please give details of the care needed and how it is to be provided)*

10. **Details of Care and other court proceedings** *(please tick the appropriate boxes)*

(a) Are the children in the care of a local authority, or under the supervision of a social worker or probation officer?

☒ No   ☐ Yes   *(please give details including any court proceedings)*

(b) Are any of the children on the Child Protection Register?

☒ No   ☐ Yes   *(please give details of the local authority and the date of registration)*

(c) Are there or have there been any proceedings in any court involving the children, for example adoption, custody/residence, access/contact wardship, care, supervision or maintenance?

☒ No   ☐ Yes   *(please give details and send a copy of any order to the court)*

Part III   To the Petitioner

Conciliation

If you and your husband/wife do not agree about the arrangements for the child(ren),
would you agree to discuss the matter with a Conciliator and your husband/wife?

☐ No   ☒ Yes

Declaration

I declare that the information I have given is correct and complete to the best of my knowledge.

Signed ...... [SIGNATURE   S F HUGHES] ...... (Petitioner)

Date: ...... 21 NOVEMBER 1994 ......

Part IV   To the Respondent

I agree with the arrangements and proposals contained in Part I and II of this form.

Signed ...... [SIGNATURE   J W HUGHES] ...... (Respondent)

Date: ...... 21 NOVEMBER 1994 ......

Printed in the UK by HMSO 803726 Dd 8262748 6/92 C2500 PP

118

What is the 'Statement of Arrangements for Children'?
This is a statement which accompanies the petition and provides information on the children of the marriage. It details the following:

- Where each child is going to live.
- The type of accommodation each child is going to live in.
- Who the child is going to live with.
- The school or educational establishment the child attends.
- What financial arrangements have been made for the child, and what arrangements have been planned.
- What arrangements have been made for the child's welfare, and what arrangements have been planned.

What happens when the respondent acknowledges the service of the petition?
The court sends a copy of the acknowledgement to the petitioner who can then proceed to the next stage, probably with the help of a solicitor. This is to apply for **directions for trial**. In order to do this, the petitioner completes a **directions for trial (special procedure) form** and also completes an affidavit relevant to the grounds given in the petition. There are separate **forms of affidavit of evidence** for each of the five grounds and a form needs to be completed for each of the grounds stated in the petition—although there is normally only one.

The petitioner will also confirm whether he or she will be pursuing a claim for costs. When all the necessary documentation has been received and checked by the district judge, a date will be fixed by the court office for the pronouncement of the **decree nisi** by the judge in court.

What is a decree nisi?
The Latin word 'nisi' means 'unless'. A decree nisi is therefore an interim stage in a divorce. It is a decree which will not be made absolute unless certain procedures are complied with. A decree nisi is made by a court but, although you will be told of the date, you will not have to attend.

When the district judge looks at the divorce papers to see if there is adequate evidence of the breakdown of the marriage for the pronouncement of the decree nisi, he or she must also consider the arrangements for the children. If these arrangements are seen as satisfactory, then the judge will certify that you are entitled to a decree nisi.

What is the judge looking at when he or she looks at the arrangements for the children?
The 'Statement of Arrangements for Children' will already have been completed by the petitioner. If the two of you can agree on what should happen to the children, then both of you will have signed this.

Even if you both agree on matters such as where the children should live and the details of the contact they should have with the absent parent, the judge still has to consider whether these agreed arrangements are in the best interests of your children. The Children Act of 1989 stresses that the welfare of the children should be the most important consideration in deciding matters of residence and contact (see Chapter 5).

In most cases, it is expected that the judge will not have to make an order under Section 8 of the Act. In other words, unlike the old system of custody, care and control, and access orders, most divorcing couples will not have an order relating to their children.

Therefore, if the judge is satisfied that no order is needed, a certificate is issued (what is called a **section 41 certificate**). The date for the pronouncement of the decree nisi can then be fixed.

What happens if we can't agree on the arrangements for our children?
If you cannot agree on what should happen with the children, then the respondent could file his or her own statement. You might disagree on where the children should live, how often the absent parent should have contact, or even which school they should go to. One of you might be wanting a Section 8 order to be made on any of these aspects.

It is important to remember that the judge will only make an order if such an order will be in the best interests of the children. Just because one of you wants an order does not mean that an order has to be made.

The judge might decide that, to get more information before dealing with disputed arrangements, a welfare report should be prepared. This will be prepared by a court welfare officer who will interview both of you, will talk to the children, and make any other enquiries that are necessary (including getting information from schools, and talking to any other people involved such as grandparents). You will be given a copy of this report. The welfare officer might include in it a recommendation as to what arrangements would be best for the children. The court does not have to accept this recommendation, but will give it very serious consideration.

Instead of asking for a report, the judge might ask you to use the court's conciliation service to see if, through discussion, any disputes can be resolved (see Chapter 4).

If, as a result, of this mediation and/or further evidence, the judge thinks that an order is appropriate, then one will be made. If, on the other hand, an order is seen as unnecessary, the judge will issue a certificate to that effect.

In either case, a date can now be fixed for the pronouncement of the decree nisi.

How do I get a decree absolute?
Once the decree nisi has been granted and, if necessary, the certificate of satisfaction regarding the arrangements for the children obtained, a period of six weeks must normally elapse before the petitioner can apply for a decree absolute. Unless such an application is made, the decree will not be made absolute. If the petitioner does not apply for any reason, the respondent can apply three calendar months after the expiry of the initial six weeks. Once a decree absolute is obtained, the marriage is dissolved and both parties are free to marry.

The moment when your marriage finally comes to an end can be anything from an anticlimax in the midst of continuing battles over property to an occasion of profound relief and release.

DIVORCE IN SCOTLAND

In many ways, the legal situation is different in Scotland than it is in England and Wales. Though there is not the space to provide a detailed account of these differences, the most significant are given below:

● You do not have to wait for at least a year after your marriage before you can begin divorce proceedings.

● Though the grounds for divorce are the same as in England and Wales, if you are using adultery as the ground, then you do not have to show that you find it intolerable to live with your spouse.

● Most divorces are dealt with in the sheriff courts. The references to the district judge in our description of divorce procedures should therefore be changed accordingly.

● The two stage granting of a divorce— the decree nisi and the decree absolute—does not apply. There is a single decree, with a short time allowed for an appeal.

● The terms 'petitioner' and 'respondent' (and 'co-respondent') are replaced by 'pursuer', 'defender' (and 'co-defender').

● The rules and procedure for legal aid vary from those in England and Wales (described below). The 'green form' scheme becomes the 'pink form' scheme, and the system known as Assistance By Way Of Representation (ABWOR) does not apply. You solicitor will tell you what you are entitled to.

There are two different types of procedure for getting a divorce: the simplified and the ordinary procedure.

The first of these is usually called the DIY procedure in that you can fill in your own forms (available from the courts or from CABx) and leave the court to do the rest. After a couple of months, you could be divorced. However, the catch is that this simplified procedure is available only when certain conditions are satisfied. These include the following: the ground for divorce is non-cohabitation for two or five years, there must be no children under 16, there must be no financial claims involved, and the divorce is uncontested.

The ordinary procedure almost always means that you have to use a solicitor. It will be him or her that will initiate proceedings by lodging a writ with the court. This writ, subsequently served upon the defender (and any co-defender), will detail which interim orders the pursuer is applying for.

Your solicitor will obviously explain to you what you need to do and when you need to do it.

PAYING THE LEGAL BILLS

Estimating the costs

How much will a divorce cost me?
It is, unfortunately, impossible to say. The divorce itself will probably be the cheapest item on the bill, unless you are going to defend it. However, the other aspects of your case can be fairly expensive: property arrangements, maintenance, any disputes over the children, arguments over contents, and so on.

Obviously, if you have a lot to fight about, you will need to use more of your solicitor's time, and you will have to pay more. An hourly rate for solicitors of at least £100 per hour is very common. Some prestigious firms, especially in London, can charge something like £300 per hour. The Lord Chief Justice has recently commented that the public regards fees of all professional people as excessive and those of lawyers as

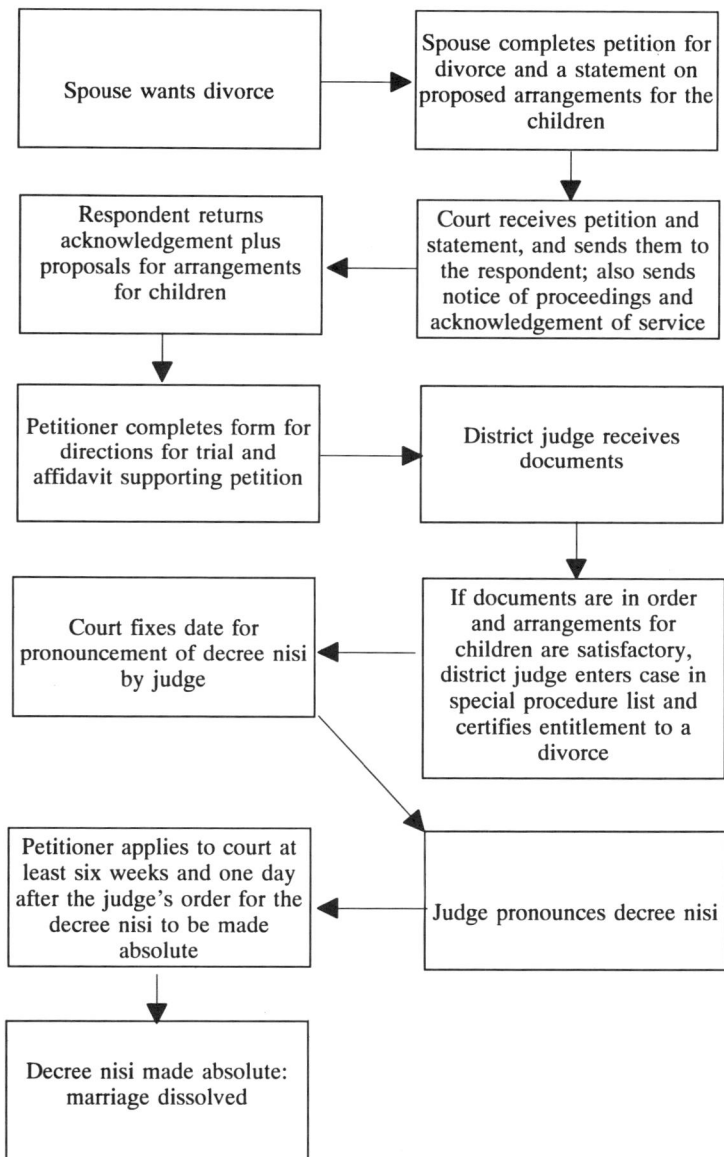

Fig. 5. The legal process of an undefended divorce, in which arrangements for children are agreed and satisfactory,

particularly excessive. You will have to make up your own mind when you get your solicitor's bill!

One solution is for legal firms to use staff who are less expensive —legal executives, for example. A senior partner in a firm of solicitors has argued that since, in 70 per cent of cases, divorce is straightforward, there is no reason for a client to meet a solicitor.

Whatever the size of your legal bill, it will probably be dwarfed by the total costs of the average wedding, estimated to be something like £10,000.

Clearly, with such charges involved, it may be cheaper to replace many minor items (a table, a chair, a set of glasses, or whatever) than to face a legal bill for the fight.

Could I pay my bill in instalments?
Solicitors are usually happy to receive their costs in stages. It may be that at your first meeting you will be asked to pay something in advance. After that, if you wish, you can be billed monthly, for example, enabling you to pay in instalments.

Getting legal aid

What is legal aid?
A system of different schemes enabling those people with low or moderate incomes to obtain legal services, such as the work of a solicitor.

What are the different legal aid schemes?
For divorce cases, the relevant ones are:

1. **Legal Advice and Assistance** (the 'Green Form' scheme). This covers help from a solicitor such as advice, writing letters, and negotiating up to a fixed amount of time. At the moment, this amount of time is three hours for matrimonial work.

2. **Assistance by Way of Representation**. This covers a solicitor's costs involved in the preparation of and representation in a case which is being heard in a **magistrates' court** (Family Proceedings Court).

3. **Civil Legal Aid**. This covers all the work necessary for cases being heard in county courts and Family Proceedings Courts. It will, therefore, include all the work necessary for the preparation of the

case and also representation in the court by either a solicitor or a barrister.

4. **The Fixed Fee Interview.** Some solicitors operate this scheme whereby you can have up to half an hour's legal advice for no more than £5.00. This scheme applies to everyone regardless of whether you are entitled to one of the other legal aid schemes.

How do I know whether I am entitled to help under the legal aid scheme?
A solicitor will fill in the application form for you and will be able to tell you whether you are entitled to help, taking into account your income and savings. If you want to check the income and savings requirements for yourself, obtain a copy of the publication *A Practical Guide to Legal Aid* (see **Further Reading**).

If your disposable income is below a certain level, you will not be asked to make a contribution to your legal services (with one exception which is dealt with in the next question). If your income is above that level you will be asked to make a contribution to the costs on a sliding scale. There is, of course, a higher level of disposable income above which you will not be eligible for legal aid.

What happens if I receive money or property as a result of the legal proceedings?
Some of it may be used to pay your legal costs. The principle is simple. The legal aid fund has a first charge on any property which is recovered or preserved for a person in receipt of legal aid. Thus, if you are receiving legal aid and, as a result of the proceedings, you lose your house to your ex-spouse but s/he has to pay you £5,000, you will lose some of that to the legal aid fund. However, maintenance and the first £2,500 of any money or property awarded in matrimonial proceedings are exempt from this 'statutory charge'. Your solicitor will be able to advise you on this.

Do all solicitors operate the legal aid scheme?
No. Some solicitors, notably in Central London, do not consider it worth their while financially to take on legal aid work. The **legal aid logo** will normally be displayed at the solicitors' offices which operate the scheme. To be on the safe side, check when you make an appointment whether the firm accepts legal aid work.

Is it true that some solicitors are introducing a scheme whereby they take on cases without payment in the hope of being paid out of any financial settlement at the end of the case?
Some solicitors are already operating this 'no win, no fee' system, although there is a statutory ban in England and Wales on them doing so. In Scotland there are signs of this system (sometimes called **contingency fees**) developing, and the Government has recently published proposals for extending the system throughout Britain.

The legal aid system does have a central problem which is highlighted by this 'no win, no fee' scheme. Many people are just above the income level below which you can receive help from the legal aid scheme, but cannot really afford to pay the sometimes very high legal costs in a matrimonial case. Paying for legal fees out of financial settlements is obviously one solution. However, until the legal problems associated with 'contingency fees' are cleared away, you are not likely to find a solicitor who will handle your case in this way.

DIVIDING THE FINANCE AND PROPERTY

This is an area which looms large in almost every matrimonial case. The divorce procedure itself may normally be fairly straightforward, but the finance and property aspects can produce seemingly endless affidavits and bitterness to match. It is not difficult to see why so much anger can be generated over the fight for finance and property:

● You are both fighting over a finite amount of finance and property; there is almost certainly not enough to satisfy both of you.

● Accusations of greed and deception are likely to be common. You may feel that your ex-spouse wants too much and that his or her affidavits overestimate his or her needs whilst understating his or her income. Affidavits, though solemnly sworn, do almost invariably present a picture of the truth which benefits the swearer.

● There is considerable disagreement amongst lawyers, divorce judges and magistrates about how to divide up a couple's assets fairly. Different rules are used, for example, by different solicitors to come up with a fair division. In Scotland, since 1985, guidelines have been used to standardise the advice given and decisions made.

● How much we have to spend and what we own to a great extent tell the world who we are.

● We resent others taking control of a central part of our lives—our income and property. It is not like paying income tax, which most people pay; in this case, it is a judge, a magistrate, and the other side's solicitor and barrister deciding what to do with your income, your house, your pension, your savings, and your possessions.

Surviving the conflict

How can you survive this process? It may not be easy, but the following factors will almost certainly help:

● a sympathetic, active and concerned solicitor
● having your interests pursued vigorously and professionally
● having a good hearing for your case
● having made some of the running, rather than simply responding to your spouse's constant demands.

On the other hand, if you find yourself bogged down in an apparently endless sequence of affidavits, none of which appears to help your case, your anger and bitterness will only increase.

The area of finance and property is so large and complex that if you really want to find out about specific aspects of maintenance for the spouse, property transfer, and taxation, you should consult your solicitor. There is a publication produced by The Consumers' Association called *The Which? Guide to Divorce* which is packed with detail and extremely helpful.

Finance and property: DOs and DON'Ts

● **Do** keep accurate financial records of income, expenditure and debts. For example, keep your **P60** which details your income in the previous tax year. An affidavit can be given much more force with a series of accompanying documents to prove your case.

● **Do** check your tax position with your solicitor or an accountant, or with the Inland Revenue. Paying or being paid maintenance can affect your tax position considerably. You might find, if you are paying maintenance, that you have to pay much less tax—but only if the maintenance is a result of a court order or a CSA assessment. Voluntary payments are expressions of generosity or concern, but are not good for tax purposes.

● **Do not** be rushed into accepting a low offer in a financial or property settlement on the assumption that a bird in the hand . . . Having accepted a low offer now, you are likely to find that a court will be unsympathetic to your request for a higher amount later. It is *you* who has to try to live on the maintenance, so stick out for a realistic offer.

- **Do not** forget that divorce affects inheritance (except in Scotland and Northern Ireland). When a divorce takes place, an ex-spouse who would have benefited is seen in the eyes of the law as having died on the day before the divorce. Children, however, remain eligible for a share in the estate.

- **Do** recognise that dependent children can make a significant difference to a financial and property agreement. The parent with the care of the children does have a good claim to financial provision for the children.

- **Do** remember that there are no set rates for maintenance for ex-spouses. Do not be surprised, then, if the amount awarded to an ex-spouse in a case you know of is significantly higher or lower than your own. This is because the court has to take into account disposable income and this figure varies from couple to couple.

THE CHILD SUPPORT AGENCY

Before the Child Support Agency (CSA) was set up in April 1993, child maintenance arrangements were dealt with by the courts and by the Department of Social Security (DSS). Levels of maintenance varied enormously, in that the courts had discretion as to how high or low they should be. There was also the problem of enforcing maintenance payments, of ensuring that the parent who was supposed to pay did actually pay.

Problems such as these led to the move to set up an official agency which would determine the level of child support according to a set formula and which would enforce the payment of orders made.

Being responsible

The CSA was set up by the **Child Support Act** of 1991. The principle that underpins it—that both parents have a legal responsibility to support their children financially if they can afford to do so—needs to be seen in conjunction with the Children Act of 1989. The 1989 Act gives both parents 'parental responsibility' and thus moves away from the previous system of awarding custody which saw some parents (normally fathers) losing significant parental rights.

The public's reaction

Despite the initial support for the CSA, the agency has come in for widespread criticism. Some of the criticisms are as follows:

- the Government introduced it only to save itself money
- the formula it uses is too rigid
- the formula it uses is too complicated
- the formula it uses sets the level of maintenance too high
- there is little incentive for absent parents to increase their earnings
- it takes too long to process applications
- it takes too long to respond to enquiries
- it makes too many mistakes in its assessments.

Some of these criticisms have been accepted by the CSA: indeed, its first chief executive, Ros Hepplewhite, offered a public apology 'to our clients for the difficulties they have experienced because of our shortcomings'. (She subsequently resigned.) The Secretary of State for Social Security also acknowledged 'deep concerns about the way the system has been working in practice.'

In its first year, the CSA saved the Government £418 million in benefit payments to lone parents. However, it was supposed to save £530 million. Certainly, one of the purposes of the CSA is to save the Government money. That is why its initial target group is those people who are claiming Income Support, Family Credit, or Disability Working Allowance.

How does the Child Support system work?

Who is eligible?

- Parents who have separated can apply at any time after the separation. You do not have to start divorce proceedings first.
- Claims can be made only for natural or adopted children, not for stepchildren.
- Both the parents and the child must be normally resident in the UK.
- If you have an order or agreement for maintenance made before 5 April 1993, then you will have to wait until at least April 1996 to apply.
- Children must be either under 16, or under 19 if still in full-time 'non-advanced' education.

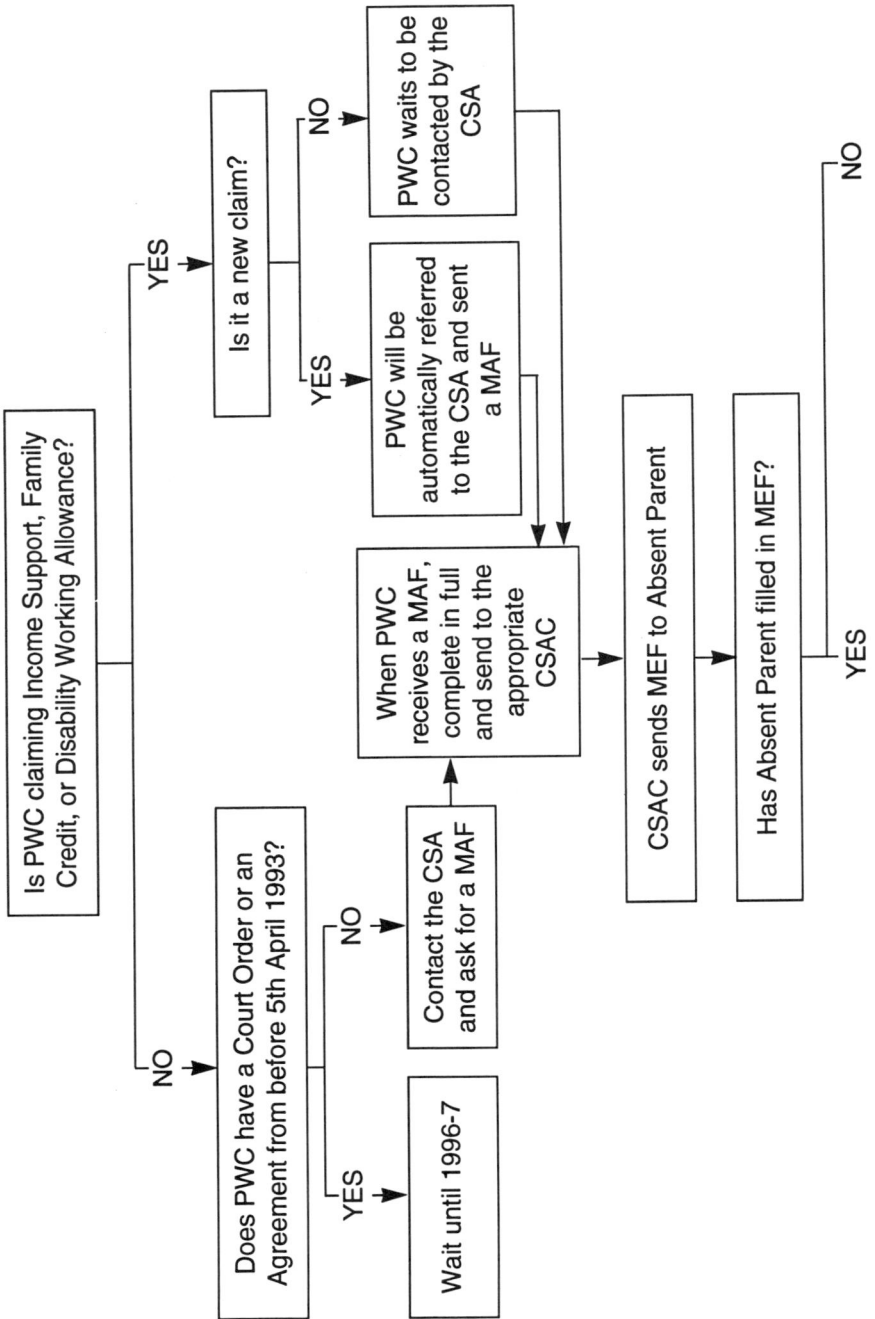

Fig. 6 Applying to the Child Support Agency

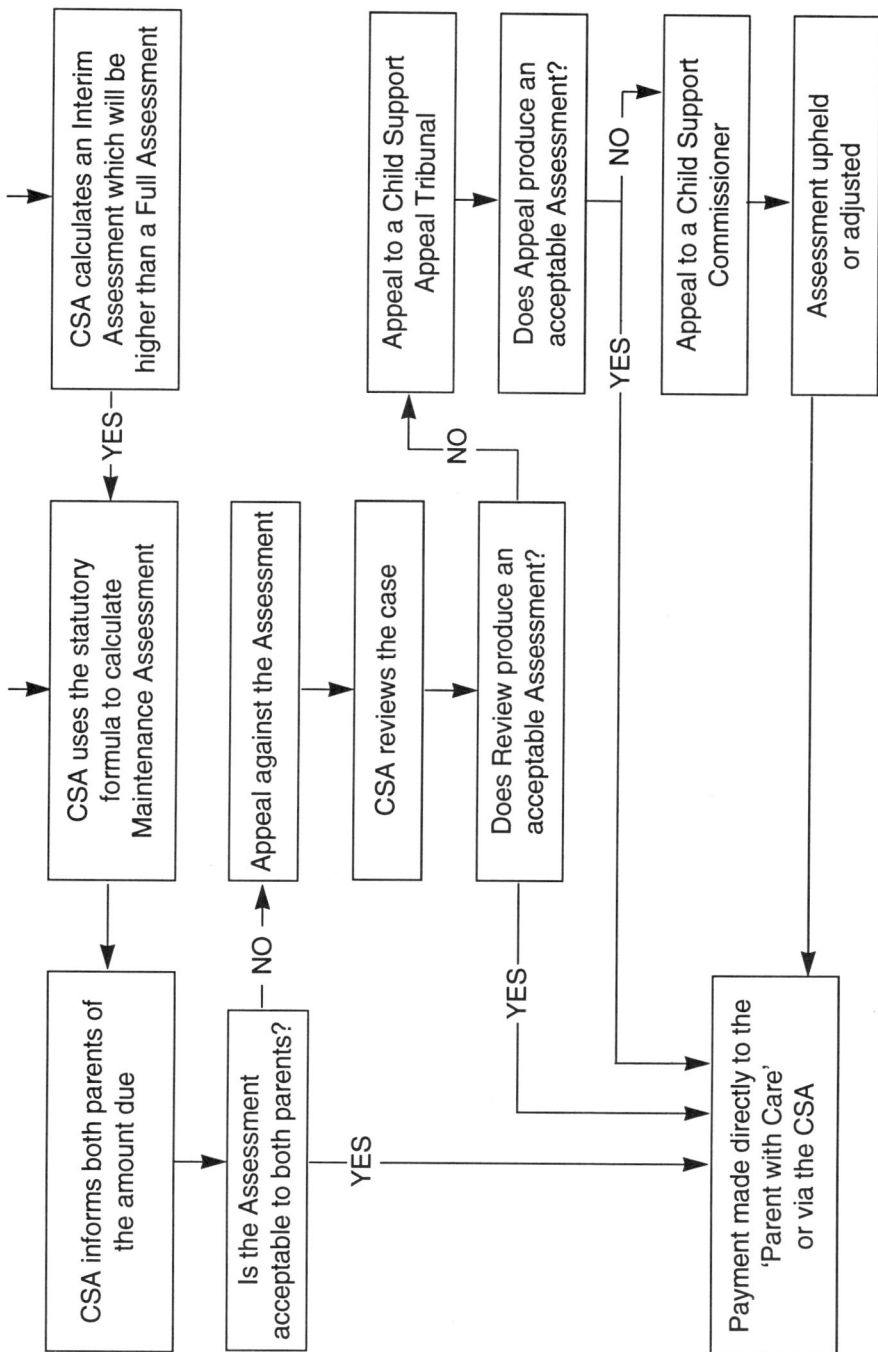

Fig. 6 (continued)

131

● People who are looking after the children but who aren't the parents (grandparents are the obvious examples) can also apply.

Applying to the CSA
Contact can be initiated at your local DSS office. There is also the CSA Enquiry Line (see **Useful Organisations**).
The following chart is designed to give you some idea of the CSA process. It is by no means a complete account of every process that you might come across, but it shows the usual stages in the assessment of child maintenance.
You will notice some curious 'words' such as 'MAF' and 'PWC'. These are used by the CSA itself and it might be useful to get used to them. They are, in fact, acronyms (each letter stands for the first letter of a word). Here is a list of those used in the chart.

PWC   Parent With Care: this is the person who will be caring for the child on a day to day basis.
MAF   Maintenance Application Form: completed by the person making the claim.
MEF   Maintenance Enquiry Form: completed by the person against whom the claim is being made.
AP   Absent Parent: the person who does not provide care for the child on a day to day basis. (In the chart, we use the words 'Absent Parent' in full.)
CSAC Child Support Agency Centre: there are six central offices responsible for the assessment process—at Hastings, Plymouth, Dudley, Birkenhead, Falkirk, and Belfast.

A number of questions might arise as you look at this chart.

Your questions answered

I have a court order from before April 1993. Can I ask the court to revoke the order so that I can claim via the CSA?
A case in 1993 in which a woman did exactly that ended in the judge condemning both the woman and the CSA for such an action. The judge argued that it was 'an inappropriate exercise' of her discretionary power to revoke the order. You could apply to the court for a variation of the original order, or wait for 1996.

I don't want to give the CSA the name of the father of my child, but I do need to claim Income Support. Can I refuse to tell them?
You can, but your reasons for doing so must not be 'inherently contradictory or implausible'. If you might suffer 'harm or undue distress' by disclosing the father's name, then you are likely to be exempt from this condition. The belief that you might suffer such distress or harm does not require that you provide actual evidence.

If you could not come up with 'good reasons' and refuse to authorise the CSA to pursue the absent father, then your Income Support could be reduced by 20 per cent of adult personal allowance for six months and by 10 per cent for a further twelve months. After that time, however, your full benefit should be restored.

I've heard that you have to pay the CSA when you make a claim. Surely that can't be right?
It is. The CSA makes a charge of £44 for the assessment of maintenance (which includes the fee for an annual review). This amount is paid by each parent unless you are on low income (including being on Income Support, Family Credit, or Disability Working Allowance) or below age 19 in full-time education. In addition, there is a collection fee of £34 if either parent requests that the CSA is responsible for collection and payment of maintenance. The exemption rules apply in the same way as for the assessment fee. Unfortunately, these are *annual* fees.

When I get my assessment from the CSA, will I have to pay the full amount straightaway?
In response to concern that people were being asked to start paying hugely increased demands without warning (including any accumulated arrears), the CSA introduced a phasing-in period which enables some payers to build up the level of their payments over a period of up to eighteen months.

If you have a second family to support, or have a maintenance agreement from before 5 April 1993 that is still in force, or a new maintenance agreement of more than £60, then you will be allowed to build up your payments to the full level over four stages. The CSA will inform you of the details if you are eligible.

Understanding the formula
'I can't even understand the formula, and I've had training in it. I don't know how the clients are supposed to understand it.' (A member of staff

in a local benefit office, interviewed for the 1993 CSA National Client Satisfaction Survey.)

The formula is based on the current levels of Income Support. Using these levels, there is a complex set of five separate calculations to produce the level of child support. Even without doing the calculations, you can be pretty sure that the level of maintenance you pay is going to be higher than it would have been under a court order. On average, the payments have doubled.

In what follows, we look at the way in which the maintenance to be paid would be assessed by the CSA. The formula is extremely complex and we use a much simplified version of it, designed to give you some idea of what is taken into account in the calculation.

Case study: counting the cost of splitting up

Jo and David were married four years ago. They have one child, Jack, who is now three. Jo gave up work six months before Jack was born and has not worked since. David is a Customs officer. They separated two years ago. He now lives in a small furnished flat while Jo still lives in their house. Since Jo is claiming Income Support, she was required to also fill in a Maintenance Application Form for the CSA. As a result, David has been contacted by the CSA about his liability to pay maintenance. What can he expect to pay?

Calculation one: the maintenance requirement

This part of the calculation uses Income Support rates to produce the weekly basic maintenance requirement for the children. You can find out the exact rates from the DSS. For example, at 1994–5 rates, the requirement for Jo and her son Jack would be calculated as follows:

Child allowance	£15.65
Family premium*	£10.05
Lone parent premium	£5.10
Parent as carer	£45.70
(Adult personal allowance)	
Sub-total	£76.50
Deduct:	
Child benefit	£10.20
MAINTENANCE REQUIREMENT:	£66.30

*awarded to those who have at least 1 child

Calculation two: net income
This should be a largely familiar calculation.

Net income = weekly gross income – less tax, National Insurance, and half of any superannuation or pension contribution.

(If weekly income varies, a figure averaged over several weeks will be needed.)

Add to the above net income any weekly amount from state benefits (such as Family Credit, but not Child Benefit.)

Also add any amounts you receive in interest from bank or building society accounts, any rent from properties, or any other forms of income.

Therefore, net income = income after deductions + any other income

In David's case, his weekly net income is £185.

Calculation three: exempt income
Exempt income is that part of one's income which will be offset against any maintenance liability. In its simplest form it consists of the following:

Exempt income = adult personal allowance + housing costs

It can also include an allowance for any child living with the parent, including both children of the previous marriage and any children of a subsequent marriage. Stepchildren are treated differently but still form part of the calculation. In addition, if you are living with a new partner, this will also be relevant in this calculation.

If you have a child living with you (natural or adopted) then you will be able to add on the appropriate child allowance plus family premium (and lone parent allowance if appropriate).

In David's case, since the rent he pays for his flat is £42 per week, his exempt income is as follows:

Adult personal allowance	£45.70
Housing costs	£42.00
Total	£87.70

Calculation four: assessable income
This is a simple equation.

Assessable income = net income – exempt income

In David's case, his assessable income is
£185 – £87.70 = £97.30

Calculation five: the level of child support
Stage 1: from the assessable income, child maintenance is paid at the rate of 50p in every £1 until the maintenance requirement is reached. Stage 2: once the maintenance requirement is reached, any remaining assessable income is paid at a different rate:

15p in every £1 if there is one child
20p in every £1 if there are two children
25p in every £1 if there are more than two children.

In David's case, he will be asked to pay 50% of £97.30 each week (50p in every £1), giving him an assessment of £48.65.
Jo's Income Support benefit is reduced pound for pound by the amount received from David. Since she was receiving more than £48.65 a week from the DSS, she continues to receive the same amount each week.

Case study: coming off benefit
Two years on, Jack now goes to school. This means that Jo is able to go back to work. She has found a job at an estate agency which will let her fit in with Jack's school hours. In the meantime, David's income has also gone up. He has already had two revisions of his maintenance contribution. Can he now expect his contribution to go down? (In the following calculation, we use the same Income Support levels, although, in reality, these would have increased.)

Calculation one: the maintenance requirement
In that nothing has changed apart from her working, Jo's maintenance requirement remains the same at £66.30.

Calculation two: net income
David's weekly net income has gone up to £201.60.
    Jo's weekly net income is £102.58 (she has no pension contribution).

Calculation three: exempt income
David's rent has gone up to £55 per week. Together with his personal allowance, this gives an exempt income of £100.70.

Jo's exempt income is calculated as follows:

Personal allowance	£45.70
Child allowance	£15.65
Family premium	£10.05
Lone parent premium	£5.10
Housing costs	£67.50
Total	£144.00

In Jo's case, then, her net income is less than her exempt income. As a result, her income is disregarded in the calculation of how much David should pay.

Calculation four: assessable income
Assessable income = net income – exempt income.
   In David's changed circumstances, his assessable income is £201.60 – £100.70 = £100.90.

Calculation five: the level of child support

   50% of £100.90 = £50.45

People like Jo would, of course, lose some useful entitlements having come off Income Support. But there are benefits such as Family Credit which might be applicable.

Case study: the rewards of hard work
Jo has impressed her boss so much with the way in which houses have been sold to well-satisfied customers that she has been given a substantial pay rise. Her net income now goes up to £184.00. What happens to David's assessment?

Calculation one: the maintenance requirement
In that, apart from her pay increase, nothing else has changed, Jo's maintenance requirement remains the same at £66.30.

Calculation two: net income
David's weekly net income is still £201.60.
   Jo's weekly net income is now £184.00 (she still has no pension contribution).

Calculation three: exempt income
David's exempt income is unchanged at £100.70.
   Jo's exempt income of £144.00 is now less than her net income. As a result, her income is no longer disregarded in the calculation of how much David should pay.

Calculation four: assessable income
David's assessable income is unchanged at £100.90.
   Jo's assessable income (net income – exempt income) is £40
Therefore, Jo and David's joint assessable income is £140.90.

Calculation five: the level of child support
Given that the total joint assessable income is more than twice the maintenance requirement, a different calculation is performed to determine David's contribution.
   Given that the total assessable income figure is £140.90 and that David's weekly assessable income is £100.90, his proportion of the total is £100.90 divided by £140.90 = 0.72.
   This proportion of the maintenance requirement of £66.30 is £47.74.
   At the rate of 50p in every £1, this gives us £23.87. With £77.03 left of assessable income, at the rate of 15p we get a further £11.55.
   The total amount payable is £35.42.

Your questions answered

I've just been sent a Maintenance Enquiry Form by the CSA but, a few years ago, I agreed a final settlement with my ex-wife in return for not paying maintenance. Presumably if I let the CSA have the details that'll be the end of the matter.

Unfortunately not. In a test case at the end of 1993, a man who had signed over his half of the matrimonial home to his first wife in return for paying no maintenance, lost his case against a demand by the CSA. He asked the court to set this divorce settlement aside and give him his share of the subsequent sale of the house. The judge, admitting that her decision was 'harsh', ruled that, though the original settlement was intended by both sides to be a 'clean break', it contained an agreement for a nominal maintenance of 5p a year for the child. As she explained, 'While the parties were free to achieve a clean break as between themselves, it was outside their powers to do so in respect of their child.' This legal point increased the man's maintenance from 5p a year to £1508 a year (£29 per week).

The CSA has increased the level of maintenance that I have to pay by 50 per cent. This means that I can't afford to visit the children for contact. Would they reduce the level because of this?

The problem with the CSA formula is that it is rigid. When the formula is applied, the figure that emerges from it is the figure that the CSA will normally insist upon. A case similar to yours produced the response from the CSA that 'a higher maintenance bill will mean expenditure choices being made. It's down to a client to decide how to meet their other expenditures and commitments.' A reduction in contact is a bad thing if both you and your children benefit from seeing each other regularly and frequently. You might have to think in terms of re-organising your contact time or making different use of it.

My husband and I have come to an agreement by which the children spend part of the week with me and part with him. It'll probably mean that I have them for four or five days and he'll have them for the other days. Would the CSA take this into account when assessing a claim for maintenance?

Yes. If you have the sort of arrangement you describe, then the CSA will be prepared to share the maintenance. However, the children must spend an average of two nights a week (104 nights per year) with your husband.

Both my ex-husband and I are on Income Support. He says that this means he won't have to pay anything for his daughter. Is he right?

No. The CSA sets both minimum and maximum levels of maintenance. If your husband is on Income Support, he will still be expected to pay at the rate of 5 per cent of the current adult personal allowance (£2.29 for 1994-5).

The CSA have just sent me a 'Maintenance Enquiry Form'. I don't see why I should co-operate in filling it in. So what happens if I put it in the bin?

Unfortunately, rather like the Inland Revenue, the CSA won't just forget you if you don't fill in their forms. If you don't return the MEF in a reasonable time, then the CSA will make an interim order which will be set at a substantially higher level than the full maintenance assessment.

I have just received my assessment from the CSA. It is ridiculously high. Is there any way of protesting?

If you genuinely think that the CSA has based its decision on incorrect or inadequate information, you should ask for a review of your assessment. If a review is allowed, it will be carried out by the CSA but with an officer who was not the one who did the original assessment. If this review does not satisfy you, you can appeal to the Child Support Appeal Tribunal within thirty days. If the Tribunal does not support you and you think that the CSA Tribunal is wrong in law, you can appeal further to the Child Support Commissioner.

However, do remember that legal aid is not available for most of this procedure, so it's going to have to be a genuine point that you're fighting for. In addition, arrears are building up whilst the appeal procedure is going on. So, by all means fight, but fight only if you think that the CSA is genuinely wrong in its assessment.

My income has dropped considerably since the CSA carried out my assessment. Do I have to wait for the annual review before I can get the order changed?

No. You should apply in writing to your local CSA office for a 'Change in circumstances' review. This can be done at any time and as often as necessary and still be covered by the £44 annual fee. Indeed, as soon as your circumstances have changed (or those of your ex-partner), you should contact the CSA in order to have an assessment which is as fair as possible.

I've just had my CSA assessment. There's no way I'm paying that sort of amount. What can the CSA do about it?

The CSA claims to follow up an overdue payment within two days, although one of the criticisms of the Agency has been its apparent widespread failure to enforce payments.

The first step would be for the CSA to write to the absent parent. Interest is charged on overdue amounts unless agreement is reached between the Agency and the parent within 28 days. This point reinforces the one made in response to the previous question about a change in circumstances.

If the absent parent defies the CSA by a continuing refusal to pay, it should be remembered that, as with the courts' enforcement of maintenance orders, the Agency can deduct the money from your earnings. Your employer would be liable to a fine of up to £5000 if a Deduction of Earnings Order (DEO) is not complied with.

If you are issued with a DEO and you genuinely believe that the CSA has not taken all the facts into account, then you can apply to the Magistrates' Court for an injunction stopping the DEO pending a CSA review of your case.

My ex-partner is telling the CSA that he isn't the father of my son. Is there any way they can prove that he is?
The CSA will offer DNA paternity tests in cases such as this. If the test shows that your ex-partner is telling the truth then his costs involved in taking the test will be refunded. If, however, the test shows he is the father and he continues to deny paternity, the CSA will consider taking the matter to court.

I think the CSA should be abolished. The whole thing is wrong.
This is a comment made by an absent parent in the *CSA National Client Satisfaction Survey*. The CSA has certainly had a stormy reception. Hate mail containing razor blades, offices on bomb alert, threats against members of staff have hit the headlines. In 1993 the CSA had to employ 40 stress counsellors to deal with its staff. In most offices, many staff are requesting transfers.

On the other side of the fence, the CSA has been blamed for increased conflicts between ex-spouses, for threatening the survival of second marriages, and even for a number of suicides. In addition, there is a prediction by the Bankruptcy Association that hundreds of people will have to declare themselves bankrupt as a result of the CSA's demands. It is likely that further changes will be made to the way in which the Agency works.

By the beginning of 1995, the pressure for change had become stronger and stronger. The very influential House of Commons Select Committee on Social Security had recommended a number of substantial changes to the way the CSA operates. In addition, a High Court judge had condemned the failure of the CSA to take proper account of the needs of children in the way it operates its formula.

The response to this pressure came in January 1995 when the Secretary of State for Social Security published a White Paper *Improving Child Support* detailing the changes which were going to be made.

● The date on which the CSA will take on cases in which the parents are not on benefit has been postponed indefinitely.
● No absent parent will have to pay more than 30 per cent of his or

her net income in child maintenance. (This takes effect from April 1995).

- 'Clean-break' settlements from before April 1983 will be taken into account.
- Allowances for travel to work (if the journey is over 15 miles) will be taken into account (at the rate of 10p a mile).
- The full housing costs for second families will be taken into account.
- The maximum level of maintenance will be almost halved from £400 per week to £250.
- Those people claiming family credit and disability working allowance will be compensated if they are worse off as a result of the changes.
- From April 1997 mothers on benefit will be able to build up a 'maintenance credit' of £5 per week which would be paid to them as a lump sum—up to a maximum of £1000—if they got a job.

The Secretary of State's intention is that these changes will enable *more* absent parents to be able to pay what they are asked. 'As a result, they will give more parents with care and their children the chance of a better life.'

Since the changes will be phased in between 1995 and 1997, you will need to check to see which has been implemented if any of them apply to your own situation.

In the meantime, if you want to get advice and support from others affected by the Agency, you can join organisations such as APART. More general advice can be given by CABs, the National Council for One Parent Families, the Child Poverty Action Group, and solicitors (see **Useful Organisations** for the necessary details).

YOUR PENSION RIGHTS

Increasingly, a couple's pension rights are becoming one of their main assets. But the courts in England and Wales do not have the power to transfer pension rights as part of a divorce settlement. In Scotland, pensions are appropriately valued as part of the couple's assets, but the courts still cannot order the trustees of a pension fund to pay one person rather than another.

The trustees of a pension fund have some discretion as to the payment of what to whom, but this discretion is limited to aspects such as payment of the pension to dependant children in the absence of a widow. They cannot use their discretionary powers to split pension rights between competing ex-spouses and widow(er)s.

For couples who divorce when they are both young (roughly, under 40), the matter of pension rights is likely to be treated much less seriously than with a couple who are divorcing in their late 50s. This would be the case especially if there were no children of the marriage.

But for couples in which the woman has not worked or only worked part-time during her married life, having spent many years bringing up the children, a divorce can have huge implications for her if she loses her entitlements to her ex-husband's pension. One solution would be for the court to order a lump sum payment to enable the ex-wife to invest for her retirement. Another solution would be for the husband to take out an appropriate insurance policy for his ex-wife.

The state pension

With regard to the state **Retirement Pension**, if a woman divorces and does not remarry, she can qualify for a pension from a combination of her contributions and those of her ex-husband if her own are insufficient.

MAKING A WILL

Case study: where there's a will . . .

Marion is concerned that, in the event of her husband's death, most of his estate will go to his former wife. Her husband Richard made a will many years ago (before she married him) and he has not got round to making a new one. He says that she has nothing to worry about because she is his wife and he has left everything to his wife.

. . . there's a way

Marriage, including remarriage, normally revokes an existing will. The exception would be where a will was made in anticipation of a particular marriage. Divorce, however, does not have this automatic effect. When Richard divorced his former wife, the will that he had already made would have been interpreted as if his now ex-wife had died on the day before the divorce. Anything which had been left to her now passes to whoever is entitled to the residue of his estate (that which is left after costs, debts, and specific bequests have been met).

Richard's subsequent marriage to Marion, however, revoked this will. Even if Richard does not write a new will, if his estate is fairly small, Marion would inherit all of it as his wife.

But he would be well advised to make a new one, specifying what Marion is to inherit. Divorce can muddy the waters of one's financial affairs in all sorts of ways. It is better to have cleared them by a will than to leave things uncertain. Where children are concerned, things can get even more complicated. It would be best to speak to a solicitor about drawing up a new will. Unfortunately, however, very few people are entitled to help from the Legal Aid scheme for this purpose.

WILL THE DIVORCE LAWS CHANGE?

'No statute, no matter how cleverly and carefully drafted, can make two people love each other, like and respect each other, help, understand and be tolerant of each other or force them to live together in peace and harmony, while they are married and living together as husband and wife. What the law can do effectively is to provide mechanisms which will protect the spouses and their children, and adjust their living arrangements and their financial positions when things go wrong.' *Looking to the future: Mediation and the ground for divorce*, a consultation paper issued by the Lord Chancellor's Department, 1993.

This sums up very well the role of the divorce laws. You can't be made to love your spouse or even to like him or her. But, if the two of you want to divorce, the law has a role in determining *how* you do it and *how* you manage the consequences of doing it.

The present divorce law dates from the end of the 1960s and was seen as a huge step forward in making divorce more humane and accessible to those who needed to take this step. However, there are many criticisms that are made about the present system and a number of suggestions put forward for changing the present law.

The Lord Chancellor's 1993 Report listed seven such criticisms.

- Divorce can be obtained too quickly, without people having to consider the consequences of what they are doing.
- There is no attempt to save marriages.
- The present system can make things worse for children because it encourages couples to be hostile to each other.
- The present system is unjust by seeming to put the blame on one partner (adultery, unreasonable behaviour) and also by increasing bitterness and hostility.
- The present system is confusing, misleading and open to abuse.
- The system discriminates between the well-off and the less well-off because living apart for two years is an expensive way of divorcing (double the living costs), forcing poorer people to go for the 'fault' divorces (adultery, behaviour).
- The system often distorts the bargaining position of one spouse over the other, by allowing one spouse to hold up a divorce.

The proposed changes

The report considered each of these criticisms and concluded that there was, indeed, evidence that the present system is not working. A number of changes to it were then proposed. The main features of these changes are as follows:

- Though the present system was introduced as a no-fault system, by using the single ground of 'irretrievable breakdown of marriage', in reality this ground has been proved in most cases by using a 'fault' as evidence. Three quarters of all divorces are based on adultery or unreasonable behaviour. In place of this fault-based system, there would be a one year process—called 'delay with a purpose'—during which all couples would have to consider all the consequences of their divorce.

- The first thing that would happen is that the couple would attend a compulsory interview at a family advice centre. Instead of dealing with solicitors at this first stage, the couple would be encouraged to sort things out with the help of trained mediators. The obvious things that would be discussed would be children and financial arrangements.

- This compulsory 'cooling-off period' would have the effect of slowing down the speed at which people can get divorced. At the moment, fault-based divorces typically take six months. With the proposed system, you could not get divorced in less than a year. However, this would be an advantage for those using separation as the 'fact' for their divorce, especially for those who have to wait five years if the other spouse does not consent.

- It is not clear what would happen if couples refused to attend mediation sessions. Though everyone would have to attend the first session, what about those who refused to continue or co-operate? Would they be denied legal aid? Whatever the answer, the Government sees the new system as costing much less than the present one. The likely cost of mediation for a couple is put at £550; the average legal aid bill in a divorce case is over £1500. As the Lord Chancellor suggests, just as we all expect to have to pay for our own weddings, perhaps we should be expected to pay for our own divorces?

However, during 1994, the Government put the proposals on hold. They remain as proposals which will be implemented if and when the political will is found.

Divorce procedures should not be designed to punish people for failing in marriage. They should, as a 1966 Law Commission Report stressed, 'enable the empty legal shell to be destroyed with the maximum fairness and the minimum bitterness, distress and humiliation'.

All those who have struggled and are struggling with divorce and its many complications would no doubt agree.

Glossary

Absent parent. This is a term introduced by the Child Support Act 1991. It refers to the parent who does not have the day-to-day care of the child, as opposed to the **parent with care**.

Access. One of the terms used in orders before the Children Act 1989. This has been replaced by the term **contact**.

Affidavit. A statement whose contents are sworn to be true. In a series of numbered paragraphs, information is given in the first person ('I left the matrimonial home', 'I have no other source of income' and so on). The information given will depend on the purpose of the affidavit and can include, for example, personal financial circumstances, the arrangements for the children, property and contents. An affidavit may be in response to one from the other spouse.

Ancillary relief. The financial and property arrangements referred to in the prayer of the divorce petition. The relief is ancillary in that it is technically subordinate to the main purpose of the petition, which is to have the marriage dissolved.

Care and control. One of the terms used in orders before the Children Act 1989. It has not been replaced by an equivalent order, although a **residence order** is perhaps the nearest equivalent.

Conciliation. The service provided by a number of organisations to mediate between couples on matters which arise during separation and divorce. Some conciliation schemes are run in association with the court, and some are run by voluntary organisations. Conciliation is especially used to deal with disagreements over children. (See also **mediation**).

Co-respondent. In cases in which adultery is given as a ground for divorce, the co-respondent is the person with whom the respondent is alleged to have committed adultery.

Contact. One of the terms introduced by the Children Act 1989. A contact order is one which enables a child to literally have some contact with the person in the order (usually the **absent parent** but could be someone like a grandparent). Such contact could include visiting, staying overnight, sending and receiving letters, and so on.

Counselling. The service offered by a number of organisations, such as Relate, to anyone experiencing difficulties in marital relationships. Counsellors do not seek to give you the answers to your problems but to enable you to find the answers yourself through full and open discussion.

Custody. One of the terms used in orders before the Children Act 1989. With the change towards giving every parent **parental responsibility**, there is no equivalent order.

Decree absolute. The final decree which fully dissolves a marriage. Once this has been granted, each party is free to marry again.

Decree nisi. The initial decree in the divorce process. It is a confirmation that the ground for divorce has been established. The petitioner can apply for the decree to be made absolute six weeks after the pronouncement of the decree nisi.

Exhibit. A document attached to and mentioned in an affidavit, detailing some aspect of the contents of the affidavit, for example, a receipt, bill, or bank statement. The exhibit (there can be several) is sworn with the affidavit.

Green form. The name often given to a type of legal aid, because of the colour of the relevant form, which gives the recipient a limited amount of free or subsidised advice and assistance.

Ground. The reason for a marriage to be dissolved. The present ground for divorce is that the marriage has irretrievably broken down. This can be established by proving before a court any one (or more) of the following: adultery, unreasonable behaviour, desertion, separation. Sometimes each of these circumstances is referred to as a ground for divorce, although, technically, they are not.

In chambers. When a case or an aspect of a case is not heard in court by a judge but in private, then it is heard *in chambers*.

Judicial separation. To obtain a judicial separation, one of the circumstances proving irretrievable breakdown of marriage must be used to support a petition. However, there is no need to prove irretrievable breakdown itself, nor is there the interim stage of the decree nisi. Furthermore, when the judicial separation is pronounced, the couple are still legally married. It is a method not often used since there is normally little point to it, except to provide a legal framework within which financial and property claims can be made.

Legal aid. A system of different schemes to enable those with low incomes to receive legal advice and assistance.

Maintenance. Payments made to an ex-spouse, usually to help towards the living costs of that person and/or the children of the couple.

Maintenance Application Form. A form issued by the Child Support Agency to the parent with care which is used to determine the maintenance requirement.

Maintenance Enquiry Form. A form issued by the Child Support Agency to the absent parent which is used to determine the level of maintenance to be paid.

Mediation. This term refers to the method of getting couples to discuss a full range of issues which arise as a result of separation and divorce. It includes a discussion of financial and property matters, together with arrangements for the children. It tends to have a broader purpose and focus than **conciliation** but the terms are often used interchangeably.

Parent with care. This is a term introduced by the Child Support Act 1991. It refers to the parent who has the day-to-day care of the child, as opposed to the **absent parent**.

Parental responsibility. This is a term introduced by the Children Act 1989. It refers to the rights, duties, powers, responsibilities, and authority which a parent has in relation to a child. Mothers and married fathers have this responsibility automatically. Other people, including unmarried fathers, can also acquire it from the court.

Petitioner. The spouse who starts the divorce proceedings by making a petition for divorce.

Prayer. The part of the divorce petition in which the petitioner requests the dissolution of the marriage, orders under the Children Act and financial support.

Prohibited steps order. An order under the Children Act 1989 which restricts in some way the exercise of parental responsibility, such as changing the child's surname.

Reconciliation. Not to be confused with conciliation. Conciliation seeks to mediate between a couple in dispute in order to resolve difficulties. *Reconciliation* seeks to bring a couple together again, to reconcile themselves to each other, and ultimately to save the marriage.

Residence order. An order under the Children Act 1989 which determines where a child will live. An order does not have to specify more than one residence, in that the child might spend part of the time with one person and part with another (split between parents is an obvious example).

Respondent. The spouse who must respond to the petition for divorce. Thus, one spouse will be the *petitioner* and the other the *respondent*.

Special procedure. Once the judge has all the necessary documents for a divorce petition, including the affidavit detailing the fact on which the petition relies, he will direct that the case be entered in the court's *Special Procedure List*. The special procedure enables the decree nisi to be granted by a judge in undefended cases with neither spouse having to attend the court.

Specific issue order. An order under the Children Act 1989 which deals with a particular aspect of the child's life, such as which school s/he should attend.

Spouse. The husband or wife in a marriage.

Statement of arrangements for children. This is a form, accompanying a divorce petition, which must be completed describing the proposed arrangements for the children.

Statutory charge. In proceedings in which a person receives legal aid, that part of any property or money which is recovered or preserved for that person is subject to the *statutory charge*; this means that if a legally aided person profits from the proceedings, the legal aid fund has a first claim or charge upon that profit. In matrimonial cases, at present, £2,500 of any property or money is exempt from this charge.

Statutory declaration. A legal document which changes a surname. By swearing this declaration you renounce your previous name and require everyone to use your new one in any dealings with you.

Taxation. Apart from its more common meaning connected with the Inland Revenue, this refers to the process by which a district judge examines a solicitor's bill and decides whether the costs are at an appropriate level for the case. If you have to pay your ex-spouse's costs and they are taxed in this way, it provides an opportunity for these costs to be examined to see if they are fair and reasonable.

Undefended divorce. Most divorces are undefended in the sense that the petition is not opposed and the fact or facts supporting the petition are not in dispute. Not defending a divorce does not, however, mean that there is no dispute over children, property, or income.

Unreasonable behaviour. One of the circumstances which can be used in support of a divorce petition. A definition of unreasonable does not exist, but it includes violence, excessive drinking, financial irresponsibility, and unreasonable refusal to have sex. This is clarified a little as what a reasonable person could not be expected to put up with.

Without prejudice. Most solicitors' letters carry this phrase at the top and, if you write your own, you should consider using it. Negotiations prior to a case being heard will normally be made *without prejudice*. This basically means that they cannot be made known to the court if the negotiations fail, unless it is with the consent of both parties.

Useful Organisations

APART (Absent Parents Asking for Reasonable Treatment), c/o Malcolm and Julie Jones, Sunnyside House, Far Lane, Waddington, Lincoln, LN5 9QA. Tel: (01522) 723240. Both a pressure group which acts to reform the operation of the Child Support Agency, and a source of advice for those affected by it (on both sides).

British Association for Counselling, 1 Regent Place, Rugby, Warwickshire, CV21 2PJ. Tel: (01788) 578328. Send a SAE for local lists of counsellors.

The Children's Legal Centre, 20 Compton Terrace, London N1 2UN. This provides a phone advice service specially geared to giving confidential advice on all aspects of law and policy affecting children and young people: the phone service operates weekdays, 2.00—5.00 pm on (0171) 359 6251.

Child Poverty Action Group, 1-5 Bath Street, London EC1V 9PY. Tel: (0171) 253 3406. This provides advice on all matters (not just those to do with children) concerning income support, including housing benefits and your rights as a claimant. They produce a wide range of very helpful publications.

Child Support Agency, PO Box 55, Brierley Hill, West Midlands DY5 1YL. Between 9.00am and 6.00pm, Monday to Friday, the general enquiry line is 0345 133 133.

Citizens Advice Bureaux, address and phone number of your local bureau will be found in the phone book. The CABs provides advice, including legal and financial advice, on a very wide range of problems in divorce and separation.

Counselling Children of Separated Parents Project (CCOSPP), Crosby House, 9-13 Elmfield Road, Bromley, Kent BR1 1LT. Tel:

(0181) 460 4606. This provides an opportunity for children to talk to a trained and experienced counsellor about any problems and questions they might have about their parents' separation. Details of other counselling and related services are also available from the same address and phone number.

Department of Social Security (DSS), address and phone number of your local branch will be found in the phone book. However, for general enquiries about benefits, pensions, and National Insurance ring (0800) 666 555. (This number will not connect you with your local office, but the service is both free and confidential.)

Divorce Conciliation and Advisory Service, 38 Ebury Street, London SW1W 0LU. Tel: (0171) 730 2422. This provides both conciliation and counselling for those who are divorcing and separating, and for those who are already divorced.

Families Need Fathers, 134 Curtain Road, London EC2A 3AR. Tel: (0171) 613 5060 (Information line: (0181) 886 0970). This provides advice on the problems of children maintaining contact with both parents during and after marital breakdown. Despite its title, FNF has both grandparents and mothers in its membership.

Family Mediation Service, 76 Dublin Road, Belfast BT2 7HP. Tel: (01232) 322914. This is the main organisation offering conciliation to couples who are involved in divorce.

Family Mediators Association (FMA), The Old House, Rectory Gardens, Henbury, Bristol BS10 7AQ. Tel: (0117) 9500140 or (0181) 954 6383. The FMA operates in most parts of the country.

Family Mediation Scotland, 127 Rose Street South Lane, Edinburgh EH2 5BB. Tel: (0131) 220 1610. This co-ordinates and supports local mediation services throughout Scotland.

Gingerbread, 35 Wellington Street, London WC2E 7BN. Tel: (0171) 240 0953. This has not only more than 300 support groups throughout the country, but also more than 20 advice centres. It also acts as a campaigning organisation.

Jewish Family Mediation Service, 3 Gower Street, Bloomsbury, London WC1E 6HA. Tel: (0171) 636 9380.

Jewish Marriage Council, 23 Ravenshurst Avenue, London NW4 4EL.

Tel: (0181) 203 6311. There are two crisis helplines: (0345) 581999 and (0181) 203 6211.

Legal Aid Head Office, 6th Floor, 29-37 Red Lion Street, London WC1R 4PP. (0171) 831 4209. Very helpful guides to legal aid and advice can be obtained. In addition, the head office will supply a list of names and addresses of solicitors in your area who carry out Legal Aid work. Alternatively, you can ask at your local CAB.

LOGIC (Love of Grandparents in Conflict), Mrs M Lomax, 9 Gainsborough Road, Warrington, Cheshire. A support organisation for grandparents involved in seeking to keep contact with grandchildren. A SAE to the above address will give further details.

MATCH (Mothers Apart From Their Children), c/o BM Problems, London WC1N 3XX. This provides informal meetings, a contact list of 'mothers apart', and a newsletter. Please send stamps or a SAE for details.

Mediation In Divorce, 13 Rosslyn Road, East Twickenham TW1 2AR. Tel: (0181) 891 6860. This is an out-of-court mediation service offering help to separating and divorcing couples and their children (and even grandparents). It is available at any stage—before, during or after separation or divorce, married or not. From time to time, they run a short course called 'Surviving Divorce'.

National Council for the Divorced and Separated (NCDS), 13 High Street, Little Shelford, Cambridgeshire CB2 5ES. This has more than 100 branches throughout the country. Details of those near you can be obtained by sending a SAE.

National Council for One Parent Families, 255 Kentish Town Road, London NW5 2LX. Tel: (0171) 267 1361. This is a pressure group seeking to improve the position of all one-parent families. It also advises individuals in need of help. It produces a range of very helpful publications.

National Debtline, Birmingham Settlement, 318 Summer Lane, Birmingham B19 3RL. Tel: (0121) 359 8501. This provides both a comprehensive do-it-yourself information pack to show people how to deal with debts, and also a unique national telephone helpline.

National Family Mediation, 9 Tavistock Place, London WC1H 9SN. Tel: (0171) 383 5993. Sixty local Family Mediation and Conciliation Services are affiliated to the National Association. Examples are

Mediation In Divorce and Counselling Children of Separated Parents Project (above). Information on the service nearest to you can be obtained by sending a SAE.

National Federation of Solo Clubs, Room 8, Ruskin Chambers, 191 Corporation Street, Birmingham B4 6RY. Tel: (0121) 236 2879. There are Solo Clubs around the country, providing a chance for divorced and separated people to meet regularly.

One Plus, 39 Hope Street, Glasgow G2 6AE. Tel: (0141) 221 7150. Provides information, counselling and advice.

RELATE, Herbert Gray College, Little Church Street, Rugby CV21 3AP. Tel: (01788) 573241. With about 400 counselling centres throughout the country and over 50 years' experience, what used to be called the Marriage Guidance Council is an obvious contact for those wanting marital or relationship counselling. Some centres also offer sex therapy and family counselling. For local centres, look under 'RELATE' in the phone book.

Reunite (National Council for Abducted Children), PO Box 4, London WC1X 8XY. Tel: (0171) 404 8356.

Scottish Council for Single Parents, 13 Gayfield Square, Edinburgh, EH1 3NX. Tel: (0131) 556 3899. From its Edinburgh head office, it provides information, counselling, and a range of publications. Local offices in Scotland provide drop-in facilities for lone parents as well as offering more specialised services. The West of Scotland is covered by One Plus (see above). Contact the head office for information and addresses.

Shelter, 88 Old Street, London EC1V 9HU. Tel: (0171) 253 0202. This provides advice and information on all aspects of housing. It provides, supports, or funds a number of Housing Aid Centres throughout the country (check your phone book to see if there is one in your area or contact the headquarters). Specialist legal advice can be given and, where necessary, legal representation. The headquarters in Wales is at 25 Walter Road, Swansea SA1 5NN, tel: (01792) 469400; in Scotland contact Shelter Scotland, 8 Hampton Terrace, Edinburgh EH12 5JD. Tel: (0131) 313 1550.

Solicitors Family Law Association, PO Box 302, Orpington BR6 8QX. The Association has over 3000 members who all subscribe to a Code of Practice which is based on the belief that it is better 'to promote a conciliatory atmosphere and to deal with matters in a sensitive, constructive and cost-effective way'. For a list of addresses of local members, please send a SAE. For a list of SFLA solicitors in Northern Ireland, write to Oonagh Quinn at Trevor Smyth & Co., Chester House, 13 Chichester Street, Belfast.

STEPFAMILY, 72 Willesden Lane, London NW6 7TA. Tel: (0171) 372 0844. (The 'Helpline'—available every weekday 2.00-5.00 pm and 7.00-10.00 pm—is (0171) 372 0846.) This provides advice, support, and information to all members of stepfamilies (including children and grandparents) and all those who work with them.

Further Reading

GENERAL

The Which? Guide to Divorce, H Garlick (Which? Books). Very comprehensive account of the legal and financial aspects of divorce. If you've got a specific legal/financial question, it's likely to be answered here but it's not a book that you need to read from cover to cover.

The Divorce Book, J Billing (RELATE). Reliable stuff from a very reliable stable.

There is a new magazine out called *Singlehanded*. This is for what the editor calls 'independent and lone parents' and covers subjects as various as the CSA, employment problems, and child care. It also has a problem page and horoscopes: something for everybody at £1.70. It is available from your newsagent.

BOOKS FOR CHILDREN

In the past few years there has been an enormous increase in the number of books which try to help children through divorce and separation. For very young children, the characters might be animals; for older children, the pain and confusion is experienced by children like themselves.

Dinosaurs Divorce, L K Brown and M Brown (Collins), cartoon book about divorce, and visiting parents, age 5-8.

Where has Daddy Gone? T Osman and J Carey (Heinemann); age 5-8.

What's Happening? Splitting Up, K B Mole (Wayland); factual, age 8-12.

My Wicked Stepmother, N Leach and J Brown (Julia MacRae Books); age 5-8.

Goggle Eyes, A Fine (Penguin) age 9+ (well known from its TV adaptation).

Madam Doubtfire, A Fine (Penguin) age 9+ (even better known from the film adaptation).
Mike's Lonely Summer—A Child's Guide through Divorce, C Nystrom (Lion); age 11+.

STEPPARENTING
Step-parents, Step-children, step by step, C Hughes (Kyle Cathie); lots of self-assessment questionnaires.
Parenting Threads: Caring for Children When Couples Part, E De 'Ath and D Slater (Stepfamily).
To and Fro Children, A guide to successful parenting after divorce, J Burrett (Stepfamily).
Preparation for Step-parenthood, E Hodder (Stepfamily); booklet.

In addition, do contact Stepfamily for details of their wide range of publications (see **Useful Organisations**)

WELFARE BENEFITS AND HOUSING
The Child Poverty Action Group and the National Council for One Parent Families both provide a very wide range of useful publications which offer detailed advice on benefits and how to claim them. Some of these are either very cheap or even free. (See **Useful Organisations.**)
FB2 Which benefit? A guide to Social Security and NHS benefits, free from DSS.
FB27 Bringing up children? A guide to benefits for families with children, free from DSS.

REMARRIAGE
'. . . I Do.' *Your guide to a Happy Marriage*, Hans Eysenck (Century). One of the most eminent and controversial psychologists of our time reviews and interprets the evidence. You may think that this is the equivalent to shutting the stable door after the horse has bolted, but it may be useful for seeing what went wrong and how to avoid the same mistakes next time around.
How to Plan a Wedding, Mary Kilborn (How To Books, 3rd edition 1995).

Index